BELINDA

THE POLITICAL AND PRIVATE LIFE OF
BELINDA STRONACH

DON MARTIN

KEY PORTER BOOKS

Library and Archives Canada Cataloguing in Publication

Martin, Don, 1956–
    Belinda : the political and private life of Belinda Stronach / Don Martin.

ISBN-13: 978-1-55263-814-9, ISBN-10: 1-55263-814-6

1. Stronach, Belinda. 2. Cabinet ministers—Canada—Biography. 3. Liberal Party of
Canada—Biography. 4. Conservative Party of Canada—Biography. 5. Canada.
Parliament. House of Commons—Biography. 6. Legislators— Canada—Biography. 7.
Magna International Inc.—Biography. 8. Businesswomen—Canada—Biography. I. Title.

FC636.S76M37 2006 971.07'2092 C2006-901813-8

THE CANADA COUNCIL | LE CONSEIL DES ARTS
FOR THE ARTS | DU CANADA
SINCE 1957 | DEPUIS 1957

ONTARIO ARTS COUNCIL
CONSEIL DES ARTS DE L'ONTARIO

The publisher gratefully acknowledges the support of the Canada Council for the Arts and
the Ontario Arts Council for its publishing program. We acknowledge the support of the
Government of Ontario through the Ontario Media Development Corporation's Ontario
Book Initiative.

We acknowledge the financial support of the Government of Canada through the Book
Publishing Industry Development Program (BPIDP) for our publishing activities.

Key Porter Books Limited
Six Adelaide Street East, Tenth Floor
Toronto, Ontario
Canada M5C 1H6

www.keyporter.com

Text design: Marijke Friesen
Electronic formatting: Jean Lightfoot Peters

Printed and bound in Canada

06 07 08 09 10 5 4 3 2 1

To my four angels,
Annette, Erin, Trina and Andrea

CONTENTS

PREFACE

S HE'S BARELY 40 YEARS old and set for life. Already well off from the $12-million pay package she collected as Magna International's top executive for three years, her inheritance will be at least half of her parent's estimated $800-million estate. Belinda Stronach will never have to worry about finding a job, paying the bills or saving for a rainy day. She has lifelong friends, fiercely loyal staff, former husbands eager to help raise her two robust children and healthy parents who, personally and financially, support her every whim. At 5'9" and a rock-solid 130 pounds, she's never been in better shape physically, which gives her 18 hours of daily energy to burn before her required six hours of sleep.

It makes the nagging question about her dive into federal politics even more confounding.

Why?

ON A COLD FOGGY election day morning in 2006, Belinda Stronach was standing at the Aurora GO Train station in pre-dawn darkness shaking hands with grumpy Monday commuters. Most of them would give anything to be at the sprawling 5,000-acre Florida farm Stronach owns but has never visited, take a break in the historic penthouse apartment in Old Montreal she rarely uses or check into her mountainside Colorado ski chalet for some serious downhill action on the powdery slopes just outside the front window.

But while they fight for a seat on double-decker railcars southbound for Union Station, Canada's wealthiest MP is shivering outside on the platform, fighting for every vote. Stronach desperately wants this day to end with her contract renewed for another four years as the Newmarket–Aurora MP. It's a $147,000 job that pays annually what she earned every 4.25 days as Magna's president, a thankless occupation that ranks down with journalists as the basement dwellers of public esteem.

She woke up that morning acutely aware her adopted Liberal Party would lose the government before midnight. Not all those rosy Conservative seat projections could be wrong at this late stage of the campaign. That meant she was fighting hard for the right to spend hundreds of mind-numbing hours on Official Opposition duty in an empty House of Commons, her Cabinet power vanquished, her parliamentary fate confined to listening while future nobodies babbled on, their words transcribed into Hansard volumes nobody would ever read.

Why indeed? It's hard to fathom. This book will attempt to make sense of the inexplicable.

SOME WILL SEE THIS semi-authorized biography as proof Belinda Stronach isn't terribly bright. No sane person who is protective of privacy would accept the research demands of the author. I required reasonable access to friends, family, former husbands, staff, her home and her private photo collection. Stronach herself would be needed for up to 12 hours of interviews with no limitation on the topics up for discussion. She would see the manuscript only upon publication. That condition put to rest what my colleagues predicted was inevitable—that the Stronach family would buy this book outright to keep unflattering content off the shelves. Even so, I insisted that an author's veto against the private sale of this manuscript be inserted into the contract. After all, Frank Stronach has managed to keep two autobiographies from being published, apparently displeased with some of his hired writers' more colourful discoveries of his past. There was always the possibility this story could end up being told his way or the buy way. Better be safe.

But no such precautions were necessary, I figured. She was going to reject my demands anyway. No one with the monetary means to buy her own vanity press publication from pocket change would dare expose her life to a journalist's unfettered scrutiny. And at the time of the pitch, she was a Cabinet minister still immersed in her briefing books. So a no-go was in the cards. And if that notoriously thick cone of Stronach silence came down over her life, it would be impenetrable and only a masochistic writer would bother to tackle the project.

Weeks of silence went by after my request for co-operation was e-mailed to her attention. She finally summoned me down to Magna's Wild, Wild West Hoedown fundraiser in September 2005 to get the final answer. It took an hour of wandering through the beer lines while watching the all-blonde cast of Hoedown Saloon Girls gyrating to the music of Jason McCoy and Beverley Mahood before I found her. Not that I was looking terribly hard. She was huddled with a friend off to one side of the massive big top erected on the Magna grounds.

"I'm leaning toward doing it," she told me, and bolted for the dance floor. Driving to Aurora from Ottawa and back again is a long way to go for that sort of noncommittal "maybe." A few more exasperating weeks went by before I delivered an ultimatum: today or never. Late that night a one-line e-mail bounced back: "You can't talk to my children. Otherwise, I'm in."

SHE HAS DELIVERED on the time and access requests to meet her end of the bargain (except for getting former U.S. President Bill Clinton to return my calls). For my part, her two children get only occasional references. Everybody in her orbit who was asked for an interview agreed to talk with a few notable exceptions. Former bodyguard Don Reeve cited a gag clause in a legal settlement for his silence. A former legal adviser declined to break client confidentiality. Former aide Tara Bingham spent six months insisting she was too busy to talk, which is a long way of saying "no." What that trio of insiders could've added to the story is open to speculation. Repeated requests for interviews with then Opposition Leader Stephen Harper and former Stronach boyfriend Peter MacKay were rejected. It is regrettable on both those counts because their side of the story cannot be fully told. If they don't like what's been written on these pages, they can assign blame to the guy they see in their shaving mirror.

But beyond those exceptions, more than 40 people talked freely about their experiences with Stronach, good or bad. Conservative MPs tended to demand anonymity before talking, which is perhaps understandable given Stronach's ugly severance from their party and acrimonious relationship with their leader. To them all, my thanks.

My particular gratitude to those who run Stronach's life by remote control and worked hard to find time for busy people to talk to me. Karen Addison, of her Aurora office, personal assistant Sheila Pearce, former chief of staff Mike Liebrock and personal adviser Mark Entwistle were especially valuable.

Calgary Herald and *National Post* editors Lorne Motley and Doug Kelly have showed considerable patience in allowing me to take vacation from column-writing duties, even when political events were shaking up Ottawa and I probably should've been on active writing duty.

Documentary producer Sarah Kapoor provided valuable insights on new ways to structure the book and make the copy flow while assisting me with her first-hand observations from covering Stronach's 2006 election campaign.

No book is written in isolation without input and guidance from the author's circle of pals and contacts. My unofficial focus group provided experienced writing direction, research help or gender balance advice. Thanks to Greg

Weston, Jenna Clark, Susan Lunn, Rhonda Cunning, Kirsten Smith, Suzanne Wilton, Gerry Nott and Melissa Cable.

My wife, Annette, and daughters, Erin, Trina and Andrea, suffered the fate experienced by all families when there's a writer in the house scrambling to finish on time. They endured a cranky guest at the dinner table on rare nights when that twisted and bitter individual showed up to mutter dark thoughts about impossible deadlines and cruel editors. Again, I promise them, this is my last book. Subject to change without notice.

But Key Porter Books editor Janie Yoon, with whom I shared a tumultuous professional relationship on my *King Ralph* book, suffered the most. She calls me The Curmudgeon. I call her The Battleaxe. Those are terms of endearment. I think. For taking chaotic chapters without warning or sequential flow and creating this hopefully coherent story, Janie has my respect, affection and appreciation.

So to all my colleagues and friends who argued Belinda Stronach didn't rate her own biography now that she's languishing back on the Official Opposition benches under her second federal party label without having any leadership ambitions, it's over to you to judge.

For what it's worth, she's got one.

Don Martin
Ottawa, June 2006

ONE

MORNING HAS BROKEN

SLUMPED INTO THE easy chair of suite 658 in the capital's historic Château Laurier Hotel, an exhausted Belinda Stronach was wavering. It was 7 AM on May 17, 2005. A sleepless night was over. Outside the window of the two-room suite where the rookie Conservative member of Parliament for Newmarket–Aurora had lived for the past eight months, another day's construction was starting on the two-bedroom, ninth-floor condominium she had recently bought in an ultra-posh complex on the most prized piece of real estate in the core. The way things were going, she wondered if she'd ever move in.

Six hours of heated argument and persuasive logic from Conservative Party Deputy Leader Peter MacKay, whom she'd been dating passionately since the 2004 federal election, had taken a severe toll on her resolve to turncoat from Conservative to Liberal. The bombshell was set to drop in just over three hours. But MacKay had planted doubt where there'd been only single-minded determination during a night-before dinner with Prime Minister Paul Martin at 24 Sussex Drive. There, she had pledged to stand as a minister in Martin's Cabinet to help preserve a Liberal minority Parliament teetering on the brink of hostile dissolution. A confidence vote was two days away, which would send Canada into its second federal election in less than a year. Her mind raced between two no-win scenarios, trying to line up the pros and cons in such a way that made the decision obvious and easy.

To go meant leaving a party she'd helped create less than two years earlier, a Conservative Party hybrid pieced together from the harder-edged Canadian Alliance and the scattered remnants of the more moderate Progressive Conservatives. She'd been a catalyst for the reunion, and she'd run for the new party's leadership just 14 months earlier, finishing second to Alliance Leader and future Prime Minister Stephen Harper as a political neophyte known only by a family name synonymous with lavish wealth from a sprawling international car-parts manufacturing empire. She'd defied the skeptics after that and run for election as a humble MP despite the leadership loss, stealing the riding away from the Liberals by less than 700 votes. She had made friends, confidants and found a lover in a party that seemed on the verge of seizing power.

The Official Opposition had a scandalized, vulnerable Liberal government in its sights as incendiary testimony of payoffs and kickbacks raged in front of Justice John Gomery's year-old inquiry into the Quebec sponsorship scandal. The temptation to take advantage of these winning conditions for electoral victory had proven irresistible to Official Opposition Leader Stephen Harper. Going strictly by the partisan numbers, Martin's government was parliamentary toast on May 19. This, Harper had decided two weeks earlier, was the window of golden opportunity knocked wide open. The Conservatives had to jump through it now or kick themselves all summer—or perhaps for all time.

But Harper hated her so. She wasn't sure why. She suspected he'd tried to deny her the party nomination for the 2004 election and had lectured her like a truant child in early May, accusing her of undermining his leadership before rejecting her pledge of support in front of her peers. She'd been overlooked in a party advertising blitz featuring star MPs that spring. A top Harper adviser held her up to ridicule at a candidates' school the weekend before, using her photo as an example of what not to do to embarrass the party. Nobody treats a Stronach this way without a very good reason.

Besides, she opposed using the proposed budget to kill the government, a move that might cost cities a promised motherlode of federal funding. There would be electoral consequences if that deal fell apart, she figured. She would probably lose her seat. And there was Quebec, where a surging Bloc Québécois looked ready to sweep the province in a spring campaign with ugly Gomery Inquiry revelations of Liberal Party kickbacks and bribes for a soundtrack, knocking down federalism and giving separatists a clear shot at a third-time-lucky referendum victory. And if those problems weren't enough, some of her beliefs and Conservative policies were a mismatch. She'd watched the caucus clapping and cheering on a few weeks earlier, eager to continue their campaign against same-sex marriage. It seemed so intolerant, so backward, so *Neanderthal*, she thought. A few days later she attended a children's fundraiser by KRG Insurance in Toronto. Controversy over the sexual orientation of cartoon character Spongebob Squarepants was raging at the time and an oversized stuffed version of the allegedly gay doll was one of the auction items.

"I've got to have that to take to caucus," Stronach vowed. She would not be outbid and, as the auctioneer's jaw fell, claimed it for $2,000.

For all of the above reasons, Stronach had promised to defect 12 hours earlier in a Cabinet-clincher deal with the prime minister's chief of staff Tim Murphy. She'd move from being Conservative International Trade critic to become the Liberal minister in charge of Human Resources and Social Development with special responsibilities for democratic renewal and implementing the Gomery Inquiry's final recommendations.

It was so easy to do. Just walk into Rideau Hall, swear an oath and sign a book. And how they wanted her and welcomed her. Paul Martin had fallen all over himself to be nice at dinner the night before. Nothing like her testy relationship with Stephen Harper. And besides, it was a sweetheart deal, a powerful inducement procured under duress from a government desperately trying to avoid a rendezvous with the electorate. Some MPs faithfully devote their entire political life to the Liberal cause and never get a whiff of the power she would grab with the stroke of a pen. It was an offer she couldn't refuse. But then there was that damn Peter principle....

Peter MacKay's reaction to her turncoat revelation had been far more vitriolic and partisan than she'd expected. She had called her father for reassurance as the argument raged. Frank Stronach urged her to follow her heart. But she'd never seen MacKay like this before. She'd hoped to maintain a personal relationship despite the severed political connection. Hell, she figured, presidential pal Bill Clinton's campaign manager James Carville had kept his marriage going strong with George Bush campaign strategist Mary Matalin, even while the pair were duking it out on the hustings in 1992 for the most powerful post on the planet. If they could do it, why couldn't she and Peter do the same? Politics is about fluid ideas, not fixed party lines, she remembers arguing.

MacKay could not be mollified. He'd yelled, argued, pleaded. *If she left the Conservatives, she was leaving him*, he'd said. It was a betrayal. A treason. Nay, the end of the Conservatives. *Good grief*, Stronach recalls thinking. *That's a bit much*. But as MacKay left the suite for his apartment, she promised to reconsider her defection decision. Now she needed time to think. Alone.

At 8 AM, trusted adviser Mark Entwistle knocked at the door with the prepared statement Stronach would read at the 10:30 AM news conference with Prime Minister Paul Martin. He'd worked overnight to write it and had quietly slipped into the hotel's basement business centre to print out a draft copy minutes earlier. A pale, shaken Stronach invited him in and immediately wondered aloud if she was doing the right thing; perhaps she should stay with the Conservatives or delay everything for a day or two.

"Think about it," Entwistle advised, having already nervously scanned the morning newspapers and found no leak hinting of Stronach's defection. "There's nothing public here yet. You can still pull out. I'll support your decision either way." He left for a scheduled meeting with Martin chief of staff Tim Murphy and communications director Scott Reid.

A few minutes later, Entwistle returned. The prime minister's henchmen had told him it was too late to turn back. A Rubicon had been crossed. Stronach stared into space for a minute, picked up a pen and proofed the statement. She wearily changed a few words before handing it back to Entwistle.

"Let's do it," she said with a forced smile.

"Okay," Entwistle smiled back. "I'll be back in a couple hours. The prime minister will be picking you up at 10:25 AM."

Stronach glanced in the mirror at the dishevelled hair, the puffy red eyes and streaked mascara. She looked exactly like someone who hadn't slept in 24 frantic hours.

"I'd better get busy," she said to Entwistle, turning toward the shower. "I look like shit."

TWO HOURS LATER, hundreds of people were sitting transfixed, staring at their television sets. Many had received an urgent e-mail or phone call as frantic friends told them to find a television and tune into a Canadian news channel. NOW. For political junkies, it had a surreal *Where-were-you-when-JFK-was-shot?* aura. Alberta MP Rona Ambrose was stepping out of the shower, her hair swathed in towels, when the phone rang. Stephen Harper was on the line to give her the heads-up on the defection and ask if she'd take over Stronach's International Trade critic duties. Senator Marjory LeBreton answered the phone to find former Prime Minister Brian Mulroney on the line, calling in the heads-up from the hospital where he'd spent four months recovering from pancreatitis.

"She's on her way to the press theatre," he said.

"Can't someone stop her?" LeBreton gasped.

"It's too late," Mulroney said.

Stronach campaign strategist Rod Love was in a Calgary hospital room where his father had died a few minutes earlier. He answered his cellphone thinking it was his sister from Vancouver on the line only to hear business partner Hal Danchilla babbling about the defection. Love hung up the phone. A horrible day had just gotten worse....

John Laschinger, a key organizer for Stronach's leadership bid barely a year earlier, got a phone call on his way to work from *Montreal Gazette* columnist L. Ian MacDonald. He couldn't believe it until Magna executive Keith Stein called a few minutes later to confirm the move and assure Laschinger that Belinda still considered him important and would call as soon as she had time.

Deb Hutton, who had been by Stronach's side as an aide during most of the Conservative leadership race, cursed out loud as she stared in disbelief at a closed-circuit television screen inside an elevator riding up to her Toronto office.

"Bullshit," thundered former Ontario Premier Mike Harris, a political mentor of Stronach's, when a client read the news off a BlackBerry in the middle of a meeting. Only later, after attending a luncheon speech by New Brunswick

Premier Bernard Lord where media shouted at him for comment as he scurried for cover, did the reality sink in.

Calgary MP Lee Richardson, Stronach's closest friend in the Conservative caucus, had just said hello to Mark Entwistle while returning to his room from a workout in the Château Laurier fitness centre. He turned on his television just in time to see a familiar blonde mane of hair disappear into a waiting room behind Paul Martin. *Funny*, he thought, *that looked a lot like Belinda*. Moments later he slumped down onto the bed as his famous friend was towed into view by the prime minister, ready to renounce her party and become a Liberal.

In Stronach's Aurora constituency office, lifelong Conservative and office manager Steve Hinder got a phone call from Entwistle strongly suggesting he turn on the television. It was, he recalled later, his Twin Towers moment—shock engulfed by disbelief. Seconds after he watched her leave the news conference, Stronach called him to ask if staff could gather at her house that night. She had some 'splaining to do, he figured, hanging up the phone. Within minutes the office switchboard lit up like the meltdown of a nuclear power station. A fury was loose in the land.

As for the guy who started it all, well, former Ontario Premier David Peterson saw Stronach off for the two-minute drive to the National Press Theatre, confided his secret to some gobsmacked business friends in the Château Laurier lobby and retreated to the same suite where the deal had been hatched through the weekend. He turned on CBC Newsworld with a gleeful sense of anticipation, anxious to catch his handiwork on the politics broadcast. He was surprised to find three talking heads from the various parties still jousting with each other over what seemed to be an imminent federal election. *Where*, he recalls wondering, *is Belinda?* Suddenly, host Don Newman cut off the panel discussion with a thunderous "Holy mackerel!" as the sight of Stronach's unlikely arrival on Paul Martin's arm hit the screen. Peterson smiled to himself at the chaos now being unleashed, the serendipitous result of a social encounter only five days earlier. Then he started packing his bags. His work here was done. He had to catch the noon plane back to Toronto.

TWO

BEING BELINDA

A PAIR OF OFF-KILTER mailboxes mark the entrance to a Bayview Avenue address on the east side of Aurora, a thriving bedroom community of 40,000 north of Toronto. A sign says you've arrived at the Adena Springs North stables. There is no indication the road leads to the Stronach family compound. Just over a small hill and not visible from the street are a security station and barricade under intense video surveillance. A bored guard coming off a 12-hour night shift grins at my curiosity about the wild parties he's seen on the grounds.

"Rarely," he says. "Mostly just stray cats and the odd deer."

What about the great golf he's enjoyed on the Magna course just beyond the houses?

"Never set foot there," the guard grins wryly. "I know my place."

He seems to keep track of the family members on site by memory. Andrew Stronach's here. Mr. (Frank) Stronach's in Europe. Mrs. (Friede) Stronach is at the house. Sorry, but

Belinda Stronach left earlier in the blue SUV and hasn't returned. You shift into park to await clearance from the housekeeper before he directs you to turn left after a massive stable and follow the winding drive into the mansion area.

The residences are numbered in the order of their construction. Residence Three is home to the only other Stronach sibling, Andrew. Two years younger than Belinda, he's something of a mystery man. Except for dabbling in a racetrack betting site featuring scantily clad women as wagering advisers, he leads a quiet and unassuming life out of the spotlight, is married to Kathleen and is father of one child born in 2001. When a slightly scruffy man at an Aurora snack stop turned to deliver a "How's it going?" to Stronach during the 2006 federal election campaign, nobody had the slightest inkling he was anything more than a casual acquaintance. That, Stronach told them later, was her only brother. Belinda and Andrew are not close.

His house appears to be a carbon copy of the mansion that Belinda had designed and built on the far side of a five-acre pond stocked with trout. Both have a stone brick centre flanked by slightly shorter grey-boarded wings and windows facing in every direction. Overlooking them both is the grandly titled Residence One. Frank's house. It is twice the size of the kids', more majestic like a European baronial estate and carpeted in Persians. A central fountain anchors the circular driveway of the house where Belinda Stronach had her first wedding reception in 1990.

The lord of the manor's not here much. The Magna International founder spends most of his time living in a small castle in Vienna, Austria, or in the ultra-exclusive

Swiss canton of Zug, where he's registered as Stronach Industries. His only wife and Belinda's mother, Friede, hangs around Aurora mostly, humbly working the gardens in summer, cooking European cuisine and ironing Frank's shirts when he's home.

But just before you enter the main wrought iron gates with stone pillars topped by horse heads of the Magna founder's estate, you turn left into Residence Two. This is the 8,000-square-foot home to Belinda Stronach and her two children, Frank Jr. and Nikki. She moved into it in 1996 after divorcing their father, Donald Walker, a top Magna company executive. It has a grandiose functionality to it, opulent without being excessive, large yet lived-in, kid-friendly while seemingly ready to host a formal dinner if the mood strikes. Stronach didn't have time to be the general contractor on this mansion like she did her expansive first house down the road, but she still supervised all the contracts and calls it her retreat from the daily grind. The five bedrooms on the upper floor create a ring around a central atrium. Linking the living and dining areas to the recreation room is a kitchen any chef would die for. The backyard has a large outdoor swimming pool for the summer, a full-sized rink for the winter. In the basement is a fully stocked gymnasium where Stronach starts her day, usually around 5 AM. The family's golden retriever, Honey, sleeps just off the main entrance—when she's not at dog camp.

On the walls of the living room hang magnificent original artworks heavily leaning toward the Group of Seven, which are the artists favoured by Frank Stronach. Two Lawren Harris originals, an A.Y. Jackson, an Edwin Holgate and an Alex

Colville creation hang under the 12-foot ceilings. Collecting art was one of Stronach's first jobs with Magna. She toured European galleries armed with a $500,000 annual budget to collect original works with friend and art scholar Denise Oleksijczuk in tow. Stronach has a bold contemporary art preference that her father, whose tastes also gravitate to carved wooden eagles, doesn't always fathom. He's questioned some of her more contemporary purchases for the Magna art collection with a furrowed brow, but invariably surrendered to her envelope-pushing tastes with a shrug.

In the recreation room are multiple sets of computers, including one Frank Jr. bought with the help of Stronach pal, British soul vocalist Seal. To help keep the house functioning during her frequent and long absences, Stronach employs a housekeeper, a nanny, a part-time cook, a bodyguard and driver, and a personal assistant.

It's all within sight of the imposing western edge of the Magna world headquarters where Stronach once held sway on the second-floor suite as president with a $12-million pay-plus-bonus package. It's a sprawling Bavarian Neverland, featuring architecture some have noted looks a bit like the Parliament buildings in Ottawa. The executive office is marked by a clock tower at the end of the laser-straight Stronach Boulevard. On the eastern side of the company property sits a 7,307-yard championship golf course with a membership that's so exclusive and limited that, on a normal weekday, only a few dozen foursomes will roam the manicured fairways. None of the Stronach family members actually golf the 18 holes, each one named after a famous racehorse. There's Secretariat, Man O' War, War Admiral,

Northern Dancer and the number one handicap, hole #4, Seattle Slew, a daunting water-lined 486-yard par 4. Having its ownership in the hands of those who don't want to play seems a spectacular, nay, unfathomable shame.

It may also seem strange in today's global village, where many parents and children are separated by provinces, if not oceans, that the Stronach family—parents, children and three grandchildren—all live within a well-struck five-iron of each other on the same section of land as the company headquarters and in the town where Frank settled 20 years ago. It's like the concept of the global village has passed them by. But that reflects the Stronach-Magna mentality. Business is family. Family is business. Best kept together.

WEEKDAYS BEGIN WITH Stronach's clock radio going off at 5 AM to kick-start an hour of vigorous aerobic activity and stretching exercises in her home's basement gym or her Ottawa condo's workout room. Breakfast is yogurt, cereal or bagels, wolfed down while she gets her news fix via morning television shows and newspapers downloaded over the Internet. If she wants an energy boost, she'll create what she calls a Super Shake from trainer Chris Smits, loaded with awful sounding ingredients like organic bee pollen, agave nectar, Vega protein and spirulina powder. But Stronach insists it tastes great.

Her days follow no set formula after she heads out the door where her driver and bodyguard waits in one of her handful of cars. She has a bevy of assistants. There's her rock in Newmarket, Karen Addison, who monitors constituency

matters. Assistant Sheila Pearce, whom she met in Grade
Four, keeps track of off-hours activity and personal appointments. Aides in Ottawa coordinate political bookings, and she
is the only Liberal backbencher to retain a communications
director from her Cabinet days, former *Sun* media reporter
Maria McClintock, to handle ongoing interview requests.

While in Ottawa on parliamentary duty, Stronach is a
fixture in upscale restaurants like Beckta's and Hy's. She
rarely dines in her two-bedroom Ottawa condo, where the
refrigerator stores only a bottle of fine champagne, a few con-
tainers of yogurt and some nuts. Her days end sometime
between 11 PM and 1 AM, depending on her nightlife plans.

Ah, yes, the legendary after-hours shenanigans of Belinda
Stronach. It's true she's no shrinking violet when it comes to
social whirling. Most nights during her campaign, volunteers
ended up in local watering holes until closing time. Her leadership "victory" bash in Toronto's Indian Motorcycle Club
was the only afterlife of the Conservative convention. And
she hosted the best hospitality suite by far at the 2005 party
policy gabfest in Montreal.

When the mood strikes, she hits the Century Club in
downtown Toronto or cruises the nightclubs on College
Street. When meeting pals like Toronto Maple Leafs star Tie
Domi for drinks, her bar of choice is in the Sheraton Centre.
But the chronic partying image seems, alas, more myth than
reality. After a dozen hours of interviews in her home or
restaurants, her total alcohol consumption was two glasses of
white wine. Most nights in Ottawa she ends up reading in
bed—alone—after dinner with friends or colleagues. And
in Aurora, she's usually booked solid to attend obligatory

fundraisers or charity events. If a blank spot shows up on her daytimer, she's just as likely to be curled up on a couch with her kids watching their favourite episodes of *Family Guy* or *CSI* than tripping off to the chic clubs of Toronto.

Those who know Stronach well describe her as an exemplary mother, although some mothers might argue it's easy to be great when there's a housekeeper, personal assistant and two former husbands to assist in maternal duties. During her frequent absences, Frank Jr. and Nikki can stay with their father, Don Walker, who lives a 10-minute drive away and enjoys an almost seamless connection between the children he had with Belinda and the two boys from his second marriage to current wife Joan. Stronach's second husband, Johann Olav Koss, also maintains good relations with her and regular contact with the children. Perhaps her description of the children is as accurate as it is affectionate.

"They're like my roommates," she says.

Their safety is a constant concern, however. Unlike her father, who usually appears in public under the careful eye of what appear to be trained killers, Belinda Stronach's security concern is stalkers. Police have been notified about a handful of problem men who seem fixated on getting to know her better against her will. She was particularly nervous after her May 2005 floor-crossing when her office received several death threats. Parents at her kids' private school watched hired guns slip quietly into position within hours of her defection.

Nothing, however, compared to the day two years ago when an Albertan drove across the country to Aurora, slipped through the security seal ringing the family compound and arrived on her doorstep. When Stronach opened to the knock at her front door, a stranger "with a funny look" barged inside, claimed he knew her and demanded to talk with her in private. Waving her daughter and housekeeper out of sight, Stronach suggested they chat on the driveway. As soon as the intruder moved back outside, Stronach slammed the door shut, threw the deadbolt and hit the panic button to summon Magna security forces. The individual was thrown off the property, but local police later arrested him. At last word he was in Edmonton under psychiatric care, but is due to be released soon.

EVEN HER SKEPTICS and critics acknowledge Stronach is a woman of generosity and compassion. She's an easy mark for charitable causes, particularly kids' and women's issues and local hospital fundraisers, but can be impulsive when her heartstrings are tugged by tragedy. After a Newmarket father was charged with murdering his wife and two youngest children in early March 2006, she cut a $10,000 cheque for the only surviving family member, a 15-year-old boy, to help with his education.

And there's no doubt she treats friends and staff well. When Sheila Pearce teetered on the brink of exhaustion at the end of helping with the leadership bid and 2004 election campaigns, Stronach ordered her into a luxury spa for unlimited treatment on her tab.

Staff report getting top-notch shirts or ties for Christmas. Key political operatives and select media (not including the author) receive massive bouquets of flowers. And she's resisted the temptation to buy an automatic signature-signing machine for the thousands of cards and letters she sends to every volunteer who has ever helped with her leadership or campaign races. She never flaunts her money, says Pearce. "She won't let you pay, but doesn't pay in a way that makes you feel poorer than her. She understands what it takes for most people and what they live through from day to day."

WHILE BAPTIZED a Catholic and married in an Anglican church, she is not religious and does not attend church, unless it's an historic cathedral in Europe or a makeshift place of worship in Africa.

"I'm not a real follower of one particular organized religion," Stronach says, "but I'm a very spiritual person. Religion might be good for some people. It gives them hope and makes their life a richer life, but it's important for people to question things. Anything that stops people from thinking independently, I don't think is a good thing."

She has eclectic musical tastes and admits to being an iTunes downloading addict. She also owns her own record label as the silent investor behind Big Bold Sun Music, an artist incubator guided by Mike Roth, the former Sony Music talent scout who discovered Chantal Kreviazuk and Our Lady Peace. That makes riding in her hybrid SUV one of those box-of-chocolates, you-never-know-what-you're-going-to-get experiences. She was an early enthusiast of the Gretchen Wilson crossover hit "Red Necked Woman," best played loud in her view, and quietly declared it her unofficial leadership theme. Another time she slapped on a vanity CD cut by a local town councillor and rocked down the block grooving to the sappiest songs imaginable, trying to fend off hysterics.

But more than her music, money, politics or boardroom behaviour, the public fixation is on Belinda Stronach as fashion template and sex object. One acquaintance confides that Stronach has spent up to half a million dollars in a banner year on clothing. Some jackets cost $20,000, some formal gowns twice that amount, they say. Hardly, Stronach laughs, she's mostly partial to Hugo Boss, although she admits to spending "quite a bit" keeping abreast of the latest trends. She started the Misura fashion house in the mid-1990s with acclaimed Toronto designer Joeffer Caoc, who created her second wedding dress, but doesn't stick with just one label.

"If I buy a suit, I break it up. I'll take a jacket and throw it on with jeans," she says. "I don't like puffy princess things, but I love blue jeans. Can I wear jeans in the House? I think technically I can. I've got a good wardrobe, but I don't take them too seriously because it's just clothes. My usual fashion statement is a simple white shirt and jeans."

She's not flashy with jewellery either, although you get the feeling those white sparkles in her spiralling ring aren't cubic zirconia. Even earrings are off limits, at least temporarily, after her pierced earlobes ripped through for the second time and have yet to heal. And while we're on her physical appearance, confidants confirm she's had a cosmetic improvement or two, but Stronach flatly refuses to discuss it.

"Have you ever had a rectal exam?" she snapped after my reluctant question on the subject. Okay, enough said.

STRONACH DOES ADMIT to several little-known love affairs, which underscore a preference for the tall, muscular, former athlete types. One was a notorious heartthrob from the Montreal Alouettes football team, a 6'2" defensive end with long blonde hair named Marc Megna. He was cut from the club due to injuries and last seen on a Florida television special exposing the lifestyles of the rich in the state. No word if that included the father of his former girlfriend. Another ex-lover was Jerome Dupont, who played defence for the Chicago Black Hawks in the 1980s. Both men remain good friends even though the romance is over, Stronach says. But the public is curious so, with some trepidation, the topic of sex was broached directly during an interview for this book.

MARTIN: Okay, let's talk about men.

STRONACH: I love them. What's wrong with that?

MARTIN: I know you love them, but how many and how often?

STRONACH: I'm single. What do you expect me to be? A hermit?

MARTIN: Some of the men in your life say you ooze sexuality.

STRONACH: Oh my God! Were they good-looking? How many shades of red am I?

MARTIN [taking a deep swallow of red wine]: I'm not sure where I'm going with this, but you are a mentor of sorts to a lot of women, so I guess I should ask the question. What are your views on sex?

STRONACH: It's great. Better than golf. What better thing is there? Is this [MP] Lee [Richardson] talking in one of his drunken stupors?

MARTIN: Um, no.

STRONACH: Let's face it. I don't sit at home and knit on Friday nights.

Here endeth the topic of Belinda Stronach's sex life.

PERHAPS IT'S THE magnetism of her megabucks. Or the Magna corporate power she had before politics and will inherit again one day. Then again, it could just be that Belinda Stronach is a fun-loving person who moves with ease through the lofty strata of celebrity society, a perfect size 6 fit with the beautiful people whose rich-and-famous lifestyle mere mortals only glimpse in tabloids or entertainment television. Whatever the attraction, friends call them Belinda's Constellation: entertainment and political stars who casually orbit Stronach's life, even if they never gravitate into a truly cosmic connection. While most tend to be male, there's no other rhythm to it, no one particular type of personality or field where they gained fame, which makes them eligible to stray into Stronach's galaxy. Musicians, actors, athletes, politicians—as long as they're fun and interesting, party on. But it's the buddy system, Hollywood style. Not terribly close. But that's close enough.

Mind you, there's nothing casual about the connection with the man who made her name world infamous—William Jefferson Clinton.

Hot or not? That is always the lurking subtext to stories where the names Belinda Stronach and Bill Clinton appear together. From the day of their first passing encounter at a fundraiser on the Magna Golf Course, the former U.S. president has been linked by nudges, winks and innuendo to "Bubba's babe," as Stronach has been derided by gossips.

The denials of a romantic liaison are effusive and there's only tenuous circumstantial evidence to back up the tabloid tongue-wagging. But there is a curious regularity to the relationship and hearing Stronach drop her latest presidential encounter into casual conversation makes it seem more routine than rare. During an interview in early 2006, I asked her if she'd had a good weekend. *Went to New York and briefly saw the president*, she said. Whoa-ah! Rewind tape. *Clinton?* What do you guys talk about?

"We talk about political issues, global issues, AIDS, poverty, Africa, trends happening in the world, the Middle East, big global issues like that. And he often asks what's going on in Canada. He has great affection for Canada and is always concerned about Quebec," Stronach says.

To some minds, that cerebral-only connection is a tough swallow. He's a former U.S. president who could call up any Nobel Peace Prize winner, movie star or national leader on the planet and book an engaging dinner conversation about a topic of his choice. And yet, he seems drawn to a Canadian university dropout with deep pockets who some see as a dead ringer for a younger, prettier Hillary.

When Frank Stronach invited Clinton to participate in a Toronto Sick Children's Hospital fundraiser in August 2001, it wasn't without a quid pro quo understanding. Clinton was looking for a donation to his presidential library and foundation. Discussing what would ultimately become a million-dollar contribution brought the president and the

Magna heiress together a couple times in the year that followed. But their paths kept crossing on other fronts. She attends the annual Clinton Global Initiative in New York, where an invitation-only seat goes for $15,000 U.S. They have seen each other at the annual World Economic Forum schmoozefest of business and political leaders in Davos, Switzerland. She was in the audience in early 2003 when Clinton was interviewed on *Larry King Live* and stood on stage when he gave a short speech before a free Rolling Stones concert that night.

"He's somebody I have a lot of respect for and somebody I think is a good person and great communicator," Stronach says. "What I find interesting is that there are few people you can relate to who makes such high-level decisions. He's done great things and there are no limits. I like people who have no boundaries, who are not afraid of taking on the biggest issues in the world."

Their most notorious encounter, backed by photos, was at an April 19, 2005 dinner following a reception for those on *Time Magazine*'s list of the world's 100 Most Influential People in 2004. Stronach had been compared to "a young Margaret Thatcher" as she launched her campaign for the Conservative leadership. About a dozen of the honourees joined Clinton for dinner at B.L.T. Steak in Midtown Manhattan afterward—dubbed by reviewers as a steakhouse disguised in a Hermes scarf—including actor Jack Nicholson and movie producer Jerry Bruckheimer. Stronach was the only woman at the table and, as luck would have it, was caught standing next to Clinton in the flash of paparazzi cameras as they left the restaurant.

American tabloid papers and entertainment television went crazy.

"She's been spotted all over town with former President Bill Clinton, a blonde bombshell who resembles Hillary," gushed *Extra TV*.

Mind you, given the show's posted biography of Stronach, you get the feeling factual accuracy is not its strong suit: "She's divorced from Olympic champion speed skater Johan Olaf Lass [try Johann Olav Koss] and currently has romantic ties to another politician: Canadian Brian MacKay [Peter perhaps?]. Still, there have been rumours of a romance between Belinda and Bill since they met five [four, actually] years ago at a charity event." All that was missing from their coverage was the usual hybrid naming of this celebrity pairing phenomenon, be it Billinda or Belinton.

No lesser authority than the *New York Times* repeated the Clinton–Stronach connection as a front-page subplot in May 2006. The newspaper produced a 2,000-word analysis of the Clinton marriage and whether its stability would be an issue should Senator Hillary Clinton seek the Democratic nomination for the presidency. It noted the former first couple spent an average of 14 nights per month together as both chased active lives beyond their New York City home. A reference was made to interviews with New York Democrats who "became concerned" at the photo of Stronach and Clinton leaving B.L.T. and the fallout in gossip columns. It was the most tawdry detail of the story and Byron Calame, the *New York Times*' public editor, weighed in a few days later to argue mention of the incident "should have gone in the trash can" as a year-old anecdote without substance.

"If tabloid gossip—like rumour in the financial markets—triggers genuine action by serious players, I think readers of serious newspapers may deserve to know about it," Calame stated. "The article didn't convince me, however, that the concerns of the anonymous prominent Democrats were genuine enough to meet my test for addressing rumours."

That the story was picked up and reprinted in Britain, Ireland, Europe and Australia weighed heavily on Stronach's mind. Sitting in a ground-floor coffee shop of her Ottawa condo two days after the article ran, she was clearly peeved that mainstream media were rehashing mere titillation as serious speculation. It wasn't good for her reputation and clearly put at risk her friendship with the former president.

"It's incredible that a golf game five years ago and leaving a hotel together after a dinner party can keep this swirling all over the world," she told me. "We're just friends. Period. When I open the paper and read those kinds of stories, I shake my head. I think people are tired of it and I'm tired of it."

It's not quite so two-encounter casual, of course. By some inside counts, they've been at the same event almost a dozen times in the last four years. And even if he's not where she is, Clinton can make sure she knows she's in his thoughts. Take the November 2003 tribute to Stronach as the recipient of a Toronto synagogue's Beth Sholom Humanitarian Award as a for instance. Guests included former prime ministers Brian Mulroney and John Turner, two former Ontario premiers, a bunch of former federal Cabinet ministers, an American senator, former president of Mexico Ernesto Zedillo and a Who's Who of Toronto's business elite.

Midway through introducing the guest of honour, the master of ceremonies' cellphone went off. It had been conveniently hooked up to a speakerphone in advance. When he answered, the unmistakable voice of Bill Clinton came over the line from China, sending Stronach his heartfelt congratulations and regrets for not being there in person. Stronach was flabbergasted and flattered.

"He once said to me, 'You're very lucky because people want to support you and people believe in you,'" Stronach recalls.

Be it true or, more likely, false, speculation on the odd-couple relationship this pair enjoys will continue to swirl, particularly if Hillary Clinton wins the Democratic nomination for president.

But there's a lot more star power than Bill Clinton in Stronach's Rolodex of global contacts.

Friends and aides say that every time they visit New York or Los Angeles with her, some famous face will walk up unannounced, throw his or her arms around Stronach and strike up a conversation like they're old friends.

Yet she doesn't boast about it and, in fact, seems uncomfortable discussing her famous friends in any detail. There's never a hint of gratuitous name-dropping. Former top aide Mike Liebrock recalls waiting in line at an Extreme Pita outlet in the riding when Stronach's cellphone rang. A friendly conversation with "Gene" ensued about who'd seen whom and when and where. Normal long-distance connection stuff. Only after she'd said goodbye with promises to hook up as soon as possible did Liebrock's curiosity get the better of him.

"Who is Gene?" he asked.

"Simmons," Stronach replied.

Liebrock had no idea his boss called the long-tongued KISS bass guitarist a friend, but it turns out she'd met him years ago at a social event and kept in touch. But there are many others she reluctantly acknowledges.

She downhills against extreme speed skiing champion Franz Weber—and can usually keep up. She's taken rocker Jon Bon Jovi to the 2003 Preakness Stakes at the Magna-owned Pimlico racetrack in Maryland where they shared a table with America Online founder Jim Kimsey, Watergate journalist Carl Bernstein and, there he was again, Bill Clinton. She's done cross-country getaways in Fernie, B.C., with Olympic skating gold medallist Katarina Witt and downhill ski champion Klaus Heidegger. She attended a private 80th birthday dinner with Pierre Trudeau, some Montreal business associates and a California mystic, who held a private session with the former prime minister away from the gathering. She was in the family and friends section of Arnold Schwarzenegger's November 2003 inauguration (the California governor and Frank Stronach are arguably Austria's best-known character exports). She's had lunch (along with 20 other people) with U.S. President George W. Bush, held meetings with United Nations Secretary General Kofi Annan, hung around with former "Ginger" Spice Girl Geri Halliwell, is friends with British soul singer Seal and had dinners with actor James Caan.

And then there's Bono.

On the evening of November 25, 2005, some 18,000 fans packed Ottawa's Corel Centre in giddy anticipation of U2 hitting the stage. In the Coliseum Room downstairs, an eclectic invitation-only group of 50 wolfed down sushi and guzzled wine at a Belinda Stronach reception for the African relief agency Make Poverty History. The gang included Liberal campaign heavyweights (who should've been working on a campaign that would start in three days and end up in their defeat), Cabinet ministers, Conservative MPs, senators and Magna executives along with friends and staff of the host who mingled impatiently with the leaders of the international crusade. They were waiting to hobnob with someone else—Bono's arrival was overdue.

Having met the lead singer through her African aid connections, Stronach had offered Bono the chance to meet the capital's political elite and press his case for Canada to boost foreign aid to 0.7 percent of gross domestic product. Stronach turned up 90 minutes late and, just as talk of a Bono no-show started circulating, the singer quietly walked into the room through the kitchen entrance.

Stronach introduced Bono, as if it was required, but barely glanced at the Irish superstar before handing him the portable microphone. Peering at Stronach through purple-tinted shades, Bono said he was "humbled" to share space with Belinda's pals.

"She's the rock star in this room," he gushed. That seemed a bit much given the speaker, but he quickly made sure everyone understood it wasn't a social call. "A sense of civic duty got you here," he told them. "What we're asking for at 0.7 is not an easy thing. It's like describing Everest and telling you where to find it. But we don't want old excuses. Incrementalism is the order of the day and I understand that, but I ask all of you in whatever way you can—in the election or whatever—to give this some momentum."

He chatted up Paul Martin's son, listened to Justice Minister Irwin Cotler and autographed an old photo of himself taken with Senator Jim Munson during the Jean Chrétien years. A quick hug for Stronach, an "I've got a rock concert to do" quip to the gathering, and he was gone. Within five minutes the reception area was empty. Somehow, Stronach had procured prime seats from a sold-out arena for the entire gang.

Joyce Belcourt marvels at the casual intersection of the world famous with the friend she taught how to change diapers as a first-time mother.

"She'd be getting phone calls from very powerful people and she'd get off and smirk and say, 'What the heck are these people asking me for?' Like Bono would call, and she'll talk and hang up and say, 'It's kinda weird, isn't it, Joyce? I'm only Belinda.' To her, all people are equal. That's just the way she is."

That is perhaps the oddest angle to Belinda Stronach. She knows her lifestyle is markedly different from most, but doesn't act like it's dramatically better. She may walk through the swankiest parties the upper crust can hold, but doesn't think anyone in the real world would find it interesting. She'll buy a $1,000 pair of shoes like most of us would pick up a pair of Zellers slippers, yet seems to be perfectly content with a cheap bottle of white wine when this lowly biographer is picking up the dinner tab. She enjoys celebrities, but isn't awed by them. If they're fun to hang around with, great. If not, well, she's always got the same friends she's had for decades who can be counted on for a good time. She is very much a citizen of two socio-economic worlds.

ONE OF THE MORE unusual and lasting interests Stronach
has shown dates back to her marriage to Johann Koss when
she visited Africa. It's increasingly a preoccupation now, and
it links to a story that suggests she is no coddled princess.

Stronach was invited by Columbia University economist
Jeffrey Sachs, the man she claims as her mentor, to take a
tour of Ethiopia, Rwanda, Kenya and Uganda in July 2005.
Sachs was developing and testing the concept of Millennium
Villages, a cause Stronach supports personally and monetar-
ily. It provides destitute villagers with seeds, fertilizer and
water to boost crop yields; storage facilities to maximize the
return on their production; and anti-malarial bed nets and
deworming medicine to keep them healthy enough to work
the fields. The theory Sachs has developed is that self-
sufficiency at ground level delivers results superior to
funnelling foreign aid through corrupt national or regional
governments. The concept captivated Stronach, who was
determined to see the experimental villages for herself. But
first, she phoned Rick Mercer.

The host of the popular CBC comedy show *Rick Mercer
Reports* had mentioned he wanted to visit Africa some day.
Stronach remembered his interest and invited him to be her
guest on the 12-day tour. But there was no private jet tour to
land beside African presidential palaces with advance teams
to smooth out logistics and a security detail to keep the riff-
raff at bay. The Stronach trio included only Mercer and her
chief of staff, Mike Liebrock. They flew commercial overseas—"I was reading *Vanity Fair*, and she's reading *The
Economist* and her ministerial briefing books," Mercer
recalls—and boarded a small turbo prop to hopscotch around

the continent following Sachs as he met with tribal and national leaders.

But when they arrived in Mekele, Ethiopia, and checked into what was allegedly the country's finest accommodation, Mercer witnessed a Stronach moment, which, to his mind, put to rest the notion of the Magna heiress as a spoiled softie.

"It was the filthiest hotel I've ever seen in my life, but Belinda didn't bat an eyelash," he recalls. "I walked to my room, and there was a thick wad of trees reaching the balcony. I checked out Belinda's room and it was the same thing. Let's not forget she's a woman and has a few dollars to her name. Anyone could climb those trees, so safety was a concern. I went over to reassure her the window was secure, but when I went to lock it, it popped out and fell onto the floor."

Mike Liebrock pulled a mattress in from an adjoining room to keep same-room tabs on his boss. Mercer took one look at his bed, spotted a few bugs roaming the stained mattress, and rolled out a sheet on the floor to sleep. Stronach shrugged at all the fuss, slapped on her track pants and a sweater and jumped into bed, bugs and all.

Paris Hilton, she's not.

— THREE —

RAISING EXPECTATIONS

BELINDA CAROLINE STRONACH was born on May 2, 1966 in Newmarket, Ontario. Neither of her Christian names have any family meaning. They came straight out of a baby book for North American kids, and her father just thought they sounded right together. Her mother does not recall her first baby's exact weight.

"I guess she was about eight pounds," Friede shrugs.

Frank Stronach built the first family home, a cement-block house, not far from the existing compound on an Aurora sideline at King Road, in the mid-1960s. It stands there still. He laughs remembering the family's next move onto the sprawling farmhouse just up the highway. Friede and the children, then aged six and four, were in Europe for an extended six-week holiday.

"Belinda went over there speaking only English and came back speaking only German," he recalls. When they returned, he took a different route home from the airport, telling the jet-lagged brood it was too nice a day not to take an extended drive. "Then I pulled into the driveway of the farm and told them they didn't have to go back home anymore. We've moved in here." Friede complained about the size, he says. "She couldn't understand why we needed such a big house."

Belinda's first memory at the farm was falling off a tractor and breaking her collarbone. She struggled home in pain and asked for a Band-Aid. Her father figured it was more than a scratch and hauled her down Finch Street to the nearest hospital for X-rays. His instincts were correct.

Life was somewhat lonely for shy pre-teen Belinda after her family moved to the farm, which featured a large bungalow surrounded by a maple forest of 1,000 trees and a pond. The kids complained there was no swimming pool because all their friends had one, Frank Stronach recalls. "I told them we had to save every dollar for the business." Her dad sometimes carried her to swim in the pond on weekends, and she still remembers the day she peed on his shoulders.

"I can't believe I told you that," she says now.

Stronach adored a pair of pet turtles, which disappeared after a prolonged stretch of forgotten feedings. Her father reassured her that he had released them into the pond to survive in a real world with other turtles. You tell her that's a euphemism for disposing of dead turtles and she's taken aback.

"So you think they really died?" the 40-year-old mother of two still wonders.

Um, sorry. Yes.

Her mother forced Belinda to take ballet for six years. She hated it. Too much practice for a child who'd much rather help the farmhands baling hay or paint abstracts or landscapes from her imagination. She was called upon to garden with her mother a lot. Too much, she says now.

"That's why I don't have a garden now," she says. "But I'm damned good at picking weeds."

Her best friend was Carol Koschke, and they'd spend weekends at the racetrack or trotting their horses on rural roads between their homes.

Many summers were spent touring Europe so her mother could visit Belinda's maternal grandparents, Alois and Maria Sallmutter, whom she calls by their Austrian designation of *oma* and *opa*, while her father's tool-and-die business flourished nationally and internationally. He'd try and join them periodically, but it was usually limited to a few days at a stretch. Friede Stronach would act as the tour guide for the travelling clan, and loved taking her children to castles and forts where she'd regale them with the medieval horrors of bloody battles or torture chambers. A generation later she'd do the same with Frank Jr. and Nikki, who lapped it up. They'd visit relatives and dine on exotic homemade breads while family members would compete to see who could serve up the best goulash and hottest horseradish. During visits to her parents' hometown of Weiz, Austria, Stronach hung around with the carpenter's kids next door to her grandfather's house. Years later, the oldest became a priest and the second oldest became a nun. The third was the rebel of the family. Belinda liked the youngest one best, and they used to make mischief in the bell tower of the town's 1,000-year-old church. It may have been a hint of her future preference for friends.

HER FATHER DECIDED to place her in Rogers Public School rather than a local private school. Nobody recalls much of Belinda in her elementary grades, including the student herself. She was painfully shy, did what she was told by her teachers and recorded slightly above average grades while spending her weekend in the saddle with her friends.

Her social side started to bud in Grade Eight. In what is almost a requisite early teen experience, Stronach's first introduction to drink was guzzling half a bottle of lemon gin and ended up with her head in a toilet, emptying her stomach under the watchful eye of Sheila Pearce.

"I can't drink gin to this day," Stronach laments.

After that, it was the usual drinks of choice for the pre-18 set: Molson Export and Baby Duck. Stronach looked older than her friends and was usually assigned the task of crossing her fingers as she entered the liquor store to buy the booze without ID. Sometimes it worked. Mostly it didn't.

She had her first boyfriend at age 15. It was a short and uneventful relationship, and she lost track of him entirely until she was campaigning for re-election in 2006. With a CBC documentary camera crew in hot pursuit, Stronach went into The Maid's Cottage bakery on Main Street in Newmarket.

"I haven't seen you since you dated Tom Murphy," exclaimed the woman behind the counter while the cameras rolled. She turned out to be the mother of her first boyfriend's best friend. Stronach declined her offer to set up a reunion.

At 14, Stronach was enrolled in Sacred Heart Catholic High School and kicked up such a fuss at not being with her regular friends, her parents quickly transferred her to the

900-student Newmarket High School. It was the older of the town's two high schools and has since been demolished, but was considered the more academically advanced of the pair. Newmarket was a lot like living in Pleasantville back then, a WASP-dominated population in a mid-sized town where everybody knew everybody by name or reputation. Crime was low, and the main industry was a Dixon pencil plant that had yet to be usurped as the town's economic king by the arrival of the burgeoning Magna International empire.

The shy side of Stronach rapidly faded in Grade Ten, much to her father's dismay. He was a strict disciplinarian, but his daughter pushed back against his authority. He tried in vain to keep a tight leash on his increasingly rebellious and outspoken daughter by imposing a strict curfew of 11 PM and threatening to transfer her to the local all-girls high school if she ignored his edict. A more frequent and pragmatic punishment was grounding her to the house, which Stronach hated because it kept her from the weekend's eagerly anticipated rendezvous with her gal pals at a roller skating rink where she'd dance to the monotonous thump of a disco soundtrack. Frank Stronach admits he had concerns about his daughter during her formative teenage years.

"At 14 they are still kids, even though they have the bodies of young women," he says. "Nobody ever got hurt because of boyfriends or girlfriends. You're just worried they don't get into any major problems like drinking or drugs. That was something I always wanted to get across. But you can't be too harsh or you won't have any credibility when it counts."

Still, there was never any doubt which parent was the authority figure in teenage Belinda's life.

"Whenever Dad was gone, I'd take advantage of my poor mother and stay out late. Usually she'd call the police to see if I had been in a car accident." As Stronach got older and more rebellious, she became more creative in her deceptions in cahoots with her girlfriends. "My friend would say she was staying at my house and I'd say I was staying at her house, and we'd have all-night skates at nobody's house," Stronach giggles.

The big blonde hair and developing figure caught the older boys' attention quickly in high school, including a motorcyclist who dropped her off after their first date and was spotted by Frank Stronach. The penalty for riding on a vehicle with only two wheels was a two-week grounding.

"She didn't lack for attention that's for sure," recalls Sheila Pearce. "But there's nothing that stands out that's dramatically different from anyone else. You date someone for a year or so and then someone else. That was high school in Newmarket in the '80s."

Despite the family's growing wealth, Belinda didn't stand out as particularly flashy in a crowd uniformed in blue jeans and rock concert T-shirts. She showed no interest in student politics, and her only extracurricular activity was the ski club. There was the monthly high school dance where "you stayed sober enough to get into the dance and got drunk enough to throw up in the washroom," a classmate recalls. "Belinda was pretty, but not glamorous. She was never the first to leave the party, but not the last one out of the door. If there was no dance and the weather was right, there'd be bush parties or we'd go to whoever's house when their parents were away. It was sex, drink and dope."

Her closest and most embarrassing encounter with the law occurred when 17-year-old Stronach and Pearce attended a bush party at an abandoned barn. Word had spread far and wide, and upwards of 100 high school kids showed up to drink and smoke marijuana while coupling in the hay bales. It wasn't until Stronach arrived on the site that she realized the barn was located on the far edge of her father's sprawling estate.

"It was a great party with lots of kids there," Pearce recalls. "We didn't peep a word it was on her property. But then the police came, and we ran terrified into the corn-fields. The next day my father and I went back and collected all the beer bottles and cashed them in."

Stronach's marks were slightly above average, boosted by near perfect marks in art, a talent that she would've turned into a career had the siren call of Magna not dragged her into the corporate boardroom.

"I was very social and wanted to go out all the time," Stronach admits. "My kids are much more structured than I was. I think I could've used my parents' guidance to force me to do homework more," she says now. "I did enough to get a good mark and be an above-average student because the teachers liked me, but that was it."

And while her marks didn't stand out, neither did her newfound status as a member of the town's wealthiest family.

"Belinda didn't seem rich," says a former boyfriend. "Very few would've known her father was that successful until he bought her a silver Z/28 special edition for her 16th birthday and rented a conservation area for the party. Most kids didn't get Camaros for their birthday."

She dabbled in recreational drugs. Pot. Hash. Nothing harder. And at 17 she decided enough was enough.

"I said to myself, 'It's not good, I want to have kids some day and I don't know what the long-term effects are.' So I quit. Many of my friends went on to continue doing it and got into some trouble."

Whatever trouble Stronach was getting into as a teenager, it was clearly missed by her mother. Pressed for insight into her daughter's rebellious streak over dinner in early 2006, Friede had to think long and hard before responding.

"I could tell you about the car accident," she grinned mischievously. Seated across the table, her daughter looked puzzled, struggling to remember what could've been bad enough to jog her mother's memory 20 years later.

Well, her mother confides in almost a whisper, there was the time Belinda was gunning her car down a road not far from the family home a little too quickly, spun out on the gravel and ended up in the ditch with two wheels mangled. Most teenagers might've been shaken up and come home, she recalls. But not her Belinda. She just phoned the house, told her mother which ditch the car was stuck in, asked her to have it towed to a garage and hopped in a friend's car to head for an AC/DC concert in Toronto.

THE YEAR BELINDA Stronach graduated from Newmarket High School, the asset value of Magna International Inc. crested the billion-dollar mark for the first time. She was officially a rich heiress. And she knew it. The graduating class party was held at Magna's new Simeone Park, a recreational complex with a lake reserved for company employees, where her parents held a barbecue.

In her late teens, with no more talk of control under a curfew, she began to enjoy the high life none of her class-mates could afford to experience. By 1986, her increasingly flamboyant father had opened a nightclub called Rooney's in downtown Toronto attached to the posh Le Connaisseur restaurant. It was, Stronach recalls, like growing up in the prime of New York's Studio 54 with Ferraris and Maseratis parked out front and long lineups out the door every week-end unless, of course, you were a celebrity or the owner's daughter and could get waved inside to a private booth without an ID check. Frank Stronach then opened a 320-seat restaurant at 1500 Steeles Avenue in Toronto and christened it Belinda's. It was a "sprawling suburban eatery with something for everyone on its expansive menu," according to a lukewarm *Toronto Star* review, which described the bacon cheeseburger as "flavourfully spiced" while the veal chop had a "strong barbecue flavour." The only notable exception to the reviewer's bland observations? "The washrooms have chalkboards which state they've been checked every half hour with a checkmark next to the inter-val," he wrote. Stronach had input in the design and a limited say in its management, but mostly just ate there when she happened to be hungry and in the area. It closed two years after it opened.

UNIVERSITY BECKONED, and Stronach resolved to leave home and get out from under father's shadow by moving to an ivory tower far from the suburban sticks in Aurora. Her father objected.

"I wanted to go away, but I remember talking to Dad. 'Why would you want to go away?' he asked me. He wasn't consciously putting a guilt trip on me, but he seemed so sad I was going to do it, so I didn't."

She opted for the closest university to her home, the sprawling and academically average York University, which was just a 20-minute drive away. She took economics, law, art and business classes before deciding one year was enough and dropped out.

"I didn't find the classes very stimulating because I had so many different exposures to business while working [part-time] at Magna. I told my parents I was going to quit university because I wanted to work. They said I should stick to university because it's good discipline. I said, 'What are you talking about? Work is good discipline.'"

Her father confides that his stern look of disapproval was really just an act. "Inside I was hoping she'd say, 'I really want to work with you.' I told her she'd have to determine that, but actually I was quite happy she made that decision."

After a month-long vacation in Italy and Paris, Stronach reported for full-time duty at the family business as the chairman's assistant.

"Watch me," the teenage university dropout told her father. "One day I'm going to be chairman of the board."

FOUR

DADDY'S LITTLE GIRL?

H E WORE BLUE JEANS into the dining room despite a Magna Golf Club dress code that strongly discourages denim. He can do that. Frank Stronach controls the corporation that built this ultra-private professional links course in 2000. That's also why he could violate another clubhouse no-no and talk on his cellphone to Austrian reporters seeking comment on the professional soccer team he owns, which just won a major championship.

On the surrounding walls, high-definition televisions monitor the goings-on in his horse-racing empire. He owns it all. The closed circuit network that carries the races. The tracks where the races are being held. Even some of the horses themselves, procured from his collection of 1,000 thoroughbreds. Perhaps, then, it's only fitting that anyone betting on his nags at his tracks is probably using his empire's computer-wagering software. The one thing missing from this closed

Magna Entertainment Corp. loop? A few more victory laps.

"I just wish my horses would win a little more," Stronach sighs.

Hovering in the distance beyond the fairways are the turrets of Magna International at the foot of Stronach Boulevard. Behind the stone façade is the $12-billion corporation's headquarters, which coordinates the car-parts production of 224 manufacturing plants and 60 product divisions with 82,000 employees in 22 countries. Thanks to his special class of super-voting stock, each one worth 500 common share votes, Stronach controls all that as well.

A clock tower marks the spot where he has a tastefully decorated office overlooking the 680-acre company grounds. Not that he enjoys the view much. He prefers to guide the company by remote control from his small 400-year-old castle in Oberwaltersdorf outside Vienna. That's when he's not picking up Magna consulting cheques from his strategically located residence in Zug, Switzerland. Or visiting his gated mansion on a golf course in Palm Beach, Florida. Or using his huge mountain ski chalet in Beaver Creek, Colorado. Or touring his racetracks, factories or merely searching the world's exotic locations for his Next Big Idea.

The once-curly mop of silver hair is close-cropped, brushed back and whiter now. Some see Frank Stronach as an older Bill Clinton look-alike. That's a tough visual to sell, but he does appear 10 years younger than his 73-year-old birth certificate. There's no disputing that he leads a frantically healthy and active lifestyle for a man of his age. Wine is a must for every meal, but he swears he's never been drunk in his life. He has never smoked, never tried drugs. He remains an avid tennis player after picking up the sport in his late 40s during a family getaway to the Caribbean. He is said to routinely put away challengers half his age in straight sets. He still skis and can bend a mean soccer ball, a skill left over from his days as a teenager when he flirted with the notion of turning pro in Austria. He has repeatedly told reporters to hold off writing his obituary 'cause he plans to live to be 150 years old.

"I was just joking about that," he says in an Austrian accent that still mangles his English on occasion. "I should be a little more disciplined on eating, though. I want to get this down a little bit." He pats the modest bulge of a stomach. "But I travel a lot now and I get off my routine. In another two years, I'll be in a lot of spas just working on my body."

More than one corporate psychologist has noted that to get the true measure of an executive, watch how he or she treats restaurant staff. Sitting in an empty Magna dining room for a luncheon interview in May 2006 offers the opportunity to secretly put Frank Stronach to the test. After my Caesar salad was delivered, he gently reminded the mortified server he had ordered one too. Then he requested, "if it's not too much trouble," a New York steak, which was not on the menu, and politely asked for HP Sauce to drown out any taste of the meat. He also waited patiently for the opportunity to order a glass of a fine French pinot noir, "liquid sunshine" as he calls it. When staff moved in to brush the white tablecloth clean of crumbs, he suggested adjourning to the bar to make it easier for them to clean up, even while they protested that our staying was no trouble. This respect-ful behaviour hardly reflects a corporate tyrant reputed to turn the Magna boardroom into his own private executive shooting gallery on a whim.

Almost everybody in senior management eventually gets fired by Frank, a former executive confided to me: "If you last two to five years, you've done well. Surviving there is like dog years, it's seven for every one for humans."

If so, well, there goes the corporate shrink theory.

Welcome to Frank Stronach's world, where money is no object, borders to business don't exist, investments are lim-ited only by his vivid imagination, and the mind is free to roam without the grind of keeping a job to pay the bills. Roughly every 10 days throughout this millennium, another million dollars accrue to his business address in Zug, Switzerland. As company founder and controlling shareholder, Stronach has commanded up to $55 million a year in personal consulting fees and Magna profit-sharing. In tougher times, that's dipped as low as $33 million—a recession-proof security blanket. Stronach says that leaves him free to dwell on thinking up solutions for the grinding social problems confronting humankind.

"I don't want to brag, but I'm very gifted, incredibly gifted," he says. "It's people like me which have input to a better society because I have no geographic bounds."

It's not just egotism talking. The business world is indeed Frank's oyster. Put in Belinda terms, he's baked a very big economic pie.

RAGS CAME BEFORE the riches in the Horatio Alger story of a boy born into poverty and uncertainty as Franz Strohsack. It wasn't easy for the first of three children and only son from the unmarried coupling of Austrian factory workers Anton Adelman and Elisabeth Strohsack, now both deceased. Growing up in Weiz near the Hungarian and Yugoslavian borders, his early years were bookended by the Great Depression and the Second World War. He lived under Russian and British occupations with irregular exposure to a formal education. His father, an avowed Communist, left the family when his son was only six. Franz took his mother's name of Strohsack and, at her insistence, enrolled as a tool-and-die apprentice in a local factory at age 14. His trade learned, he became restless in postwar Europe and, despite the offer of a professional soccer position, the ambitious 22-year-old opted to join the mass migration overseas. The year was 1954. He had $200 in his pocket. He set sail from Germany under the made-for-Canada name of Frank Stronach and arrived with all his worldly possessions crammed into a suitcase that would easily qualify today as airline carry-aboard baggage.

He was dropped off on a Quebec City wharf and, being able to speak a little English, was handed a train ticket to Montreal by a skeptical immigration officer who wished him luck.

"I arrived at this huge railway station in Montreal with this little suitcase, and I walked along the road until I asked someone where to find cheap rooms for rent," he recalls.

Quickly lost, he wandered for another hour or two until he stumbled upon the city's seedy rooming-house district, booked a bed and set out to find a job. It was a recession year and regular work was tough to find, particularly for someone with limited English skills coming straight off the boat. He was told about a day job retrieving golf balls at a driving range.

"I drove a whole day up and down the street on a bus looking for it, but little did I know that golf courses usually weren't on bus routes," he reflects. "If I'd found the place, you sometimes wonder if my life might've been one of the great famous golfers."

Desperate and down to his last $40, Stronach bought a one-way Greyhound bus ticket to Kitchener, Ontario. In his pocket was one last lifeline, a scrap of paper with the scribbled address of another former Weiz acquaintance who had emigrated to Canada's Oktoberfest capital two years earlier. Hungry, homeless, tired and scared, Stronach got off the bus and hoped like hell his contact hadn't moved to another city in the last few months. After an hour's walk from the bus station, he knocked hesitantly on the door and held his breath. It opened and a familiar face peered out and gasped, "You look rough. Come on in."

Within the week, Stronach had his first job in Canada—washing dishes in the Kitchener hospital.

Three years later, he had saved enough money to partner with boyhood friend Anton Czapka and open Multimatic Tool and Die in a garage on Toronto's Dupont Street. He spent months sleeping on a cot beside the lathe, the better to save on rent money for the fledgling business. Stronach recalls cutting his bare feet on metal shavings whenever he was forced to get up in the middle of the night to use the only available washroom in the shop next door. Working 16-hour days with no weekends or holidays off and reinvesting almost all of their earnings in the shop, the partners quickly earned a reputation for delivering low-priced, high-quality product on time. The shop had 10 full-time employees at the end of their first year in business. They glimpsed a future in making small components for major automobile manufacturers at a price the Big Three couldn't match on their own. The fledgling company's first major deal was in 1959, a $30,000 contract to supply sun visor brackets to General Motors of Canada Ltd. With that delivery, a theory was put into practice; a niche was discovered; an empire was born. It took Frank Stronach less than 10 years to parlay the pittance he arrived with, an amount that wouldn't even pay for a round of golf at his company's course today, into his first million.

As the business flourished at the dawn of the 1960s, Stronach decided to splurge on a little gloating in his native country. He shipped a luxury-loaded Pontiac convertible by boat to Germany and drove it through the Alps, parading through the streets of Weiz with the top down like some hero returning home after conquering the New World.

The second time he travelled to his homeland, it was on a more serious mission. In 1962, Stronach went searching for a woman with the right genes to become the mother of his children. He spotted gorgeous 18-year-old Elfriede Sallmutter whipping down a ski hill and gave chase. Love was a secondary consideration, but he wooed her shamelessly and two years later sent her a one-way airline ticket to Toronto. Over her parents' objections, Elfriede used it. A few months later in early 1965, Stronach's self-arranged union was given a priest's blessing in a Toronto church.

"It was planned," Stronach freely admits of his marriage. "I wasn't sure in my mid-30s that I would stay in Canada. So I figured I would like to have kids, but if I married a Canadian and wanted to go back to Austria...I don't know. This was a great lady from a great family with great character. She's very down to earth, very intelligent. I wasn't overly in love with her, but I just felt like having kids. It was as simple as that—I wanted to have kids."

So did Elfriede Sallmutter deliver adequately on the bargain that brought her to Canada? "She's been okay to have kids with," he shrugs.

A year after the nuptials, Belinda was born. Two years later, the sought-after son arrived. The father was ecstatic that Magna had its rightful male heir. Andy Stronach would prove to have different ideas.

"I think he loves her," allows Belinda Stronach when asked about her parents' curious self-arranged marriage, their lives separated by the Atlantic Ocean for most of the year. "I've seen where he's been there to support her, and he has a lot of respect for her and for her character."

She's heard the stories of her father's appreciative eye for other women and seen his flirtations on public display when he hit the dance floor surrounded by beautiful girls at Rooney's, the nightclub he owned in Toronto. But she refuses to be judgmental.

"The older you get, the more you realize your parents are human," she sighs. "They've got their strengths and weaknesses just like everybody else, and they have to determine what arrangement makes them happy. You've got to accept them for what they are."

Elfriede Stronach is, by all accounts, her husband's polar opposite. Blonde and slim with lingering signs of the youthful beauty that captured her husband's attention, she's an island of down-to-earth calm in a family of whirlwind-driven whitecaps. While her husband gallivants, she gardens. On those rare days he's in Aurora, she cooks for him, irons his shirts and does the laundry. When guests arrive, her first question is invariably whether they've eaten recently. If not, she'll hit the kitchen to whip up a sandwich. Bring her a token host gift and visitors say they are profusely thanked. Her role in the family business is confined to the horses, both in the family estate's massive stable and throughout North America, but she'd much rather work in her garden and leave the nag business to others.

Perhaps the best insight into the gentle, mysterious matriarch of the Stronach family occurred on the day a former U.S. president came to visit in 2001. Bill Clinton was speaking at a fundraising event after a round of golf on the Magna course and needed a place to change for his speech. Secret service agents swept the mansion for security risks and asked where they could find an iron to press Clinton's shirt. Elfriede wouldn't hear of it. *She* would iron out the presidential wrinkles. Unfortunately while doing so, she popped off a button. While a bemused Clinton waited in his undershirt, she calmly sewed it back on.

The other unknown in the Stronach family is Andy, born in 1968 and bred for success as the male heir. Old European attitudes die hard, so it's not surprising that a wife-shopping Stronach would prefer his son to follow in his masculine footsteps. Daughters, Stronach figured, stay home, cook, clean and keep their husbands happy. It would prove to be the one part of his carefully choreographed life that didn't turn out as planned.

Belinda and Andy weren't particularly close throughout their upbringing. There just wasn't enough compatible DNA to form a sibling bond. They'd sit together over dinners. They'd tolerate each other during the forced confinement of family vacations. Beyond that, they shared only an address, not a life.

Andy spent the summers of his youth at private tennis camps and excelled at the sport, but showed little interest in the car-parts side of the family business. While his sister was horseback riding, rollerskating and necking at bush parties before growing into the nightclub scene, Andy was quietly returning tennis balls and memorizing horse racing guides, gaining an encyclopedic knowledge of racehorses and their bloodlines.

Family and friends arch their eyebrows and lower their discretion when asked about Andy Stronach today, who is married with a daughter, Celina, born in 2001. He's "odd," some say. Ordinary looks. Quiet personality. Nice guy. Last seen taking guitar lessons at the local music conservatory. Nothing like Belinda. Andy's introversion is invariably linked by outsiders to growing up under a demanding father's long and impossible-to-please shadow. Surprisingly, Frank Stronach agrees.

"It's more difficult for a son if the father has been successful," Stronach admits. "If I could do it over again, I wouldn't be tough on the kid. He was a boy. I was stricter, maybe tougher. With Belinda I wasn't strict. I just told her I loved her and to be careful."

"I had a different kind of pressure," Belinda Stronach responds. She was the modern cosmopolitan woman trying to convince her father his old ways were relics of societal history. "You're expected to be a good cook and a good mother, and that's when I said, 'Screw you, I'm not doing that,'" she says. "Yes, it's important to be a good cook and a good mother, but I want a hell of a lot more out of life."

SUCCESSION PLANNING has always been a simmering preoccupation for Frank Stronach. He's determined to will his trust-held shares, which wield effective control over the company, to someone he believes will pledge allegiance to Magna's unique profit-sharing commitments and corporate philanthropy. Yet even directors on the board know Magna will always stay under family control. And that leaves only two heir-raising possibilities.

"You hope for a son when you have something to give over," Frank Stronach says. There's a rueful pause. "Andy said, 'Look, I don't need you. I can do my own thing.' It's more difficult."

By "difficult" he means accepting a female as his replacement, even if that means waiting until she gets the political itch out of her system.

"I had to break through the barrier of saying, 'I can do this job and better than anybody else,'" Belinda recalls now. "He [Andy] had the pressure of having a very successful father. In some ways I had no expectations, and I had to burst through that while he had lots of expectations."

Questions persist about Andy's place in the empire after his apparent severance from Magna under bad terms. When pressed on where his son fits in company plans, Frank Stronach becomes uncharacteristically circumspect amid brooding hints of deeper problems.

"When you run a public company you must be very rigid. The rules and the laws are very tough. You could jeopardize a big company." He pauses. "You need ironclad rules," he repeats. "He [Andy] was more of a rebel. He was more free-spirited, so the spirit you have to temper in a public company."

Stronach does not care to elaborate, but Andy's free spirit appears to have culminated in his departure from Magna Entertainment in 2002 to start Futuristic Entertainment Holdings Inc. The company planned to build a user-friendly touch-screen machine to help amateurs place their bets at the track. Those close to the family confide that bad blood was spilled over the proprietary rights to the software—Frank Stronach insisted it was Magna technology while Andy Stronach argued it belonged to him. While there's been talk of testing the machines, tentatively called Hot Walkers because they feature women in skimpy outfits, the status of the technology as a going concern is unclear.

A related concept involving Andy was Shetips.com, a Web site serving up attractive women to promote horse-betting picks for paying clients over the Internet. Belinda Stronach abhorred the concept and joined a chorus of complaints in the racing fraternity to protest the technology as sexist.

"I've made my views known. I don't like it," she says. "But I'm not my brother. He has to make his choices."

Shetips.com appeared to be in trouble at this writing. The Web site has been mothballed with a posted promise to relaunch at an unspecified future date. Clients can request a transfer or refund of their credit balances.

As you may have gathered by now, there's an aura of dysfunctionality to the Stronachs as a family unit. The long-distance marriage of a man to a woman he selected for her reproductive potential is clearly unusual. And while brother and sister can wave across the pond to each other and Andy's five-year-old daughter can wander unannounced into her aunt's home looking for playmates, the two siblings never socialize beyond obligatory family get-togethers. As they were as youngsters, they remain closely related strangers to this day.

THROUGH THE GLORY years of the 1980s with company growth and sales skyrocketing, Frank Stronach gained considerable public notoriety for his whimsical imagination. His annual compensation package soared over $2 million, making him the highest-paid company executive in Canada. He wasn't shy about spending his wealth.

He launched what was supposed to become a family restaurant chain called Belinda's, opened an upscale Toronto nightclub, started a tennis clothing operation, published a short-lived "alternative business magazine" called *Vista* and blew $8 million building a bug-like car called the Torreno with a $200,000 (in 1988 dollars) sticker price that was never mass produced. And then there was his most grandiose idea that never got off the ground, literally or financially: Magna Air.

It was something Frank Stronach could see himself using, so he figured it had to be a winning concept. He announced plans to lease two Airbus A319s, which would be stripped down to 30 seats and turned into a flying Taj Mahal. Each seat would be surrounded by a bed and office equipment for the ultra-discriminating business pond-jumper. Showers were included, secretaries were not. But while Stronach was pushing the concept in Europe, his Aurora management team was doing a full reverse thrust at home, insisting the idea was very much grounded at conception. After purchasing rights to lease the planes, Magna directors quietly let the options lapse. The shareholders were relieved.

In 1988, his imagination weary from so many wild initiatives beyond the car-parts business, Stronach embarked on a new challenge. He decided to apply for membership in an exclusive country club with just 295 members: the House of Commons.

He made a strange choice of riding and party affiliation in his bid to become the member of Parliament for York–Simcoe. In the heart of then-Conservative country north of Toronto, he ran for John Turner's Liberals, who were attempting a comeback after their severe spanking from Brian Mulroney's 1984 majority. Even more confounding was that the Liberals were campaigning on a single issue: their angry opposition to the North American Free Trade Agreement. Having a global industrialist running on an anti-free-trade platform seems about as far-fetched as current Prime Minister Stephen Harper campaigning in favour of a larger and more aggressive national press gallery.

"There's no such thing as free trade," Stronach argues now. "Did you ever play marbles in the schoolyard? I played once against this big guy and won the marbles and he said, 'Don't you know the latest rules?' I was a smart kid and I gave the marbles back. That's how free trade works. The biggest guy wins. I prefer fair trade."

Beyond his strange party pick was the irony of having incumbent Conservative MP Sinclair Stevens as his initial campaign rival. The former Industry minister had been the subject of a conflict of interest inquiry after his wife, Noreen, borrowed $2.6 million from a consultant who had done business with her husband's ministerial department. The company employing that consultant? Magna International.

Stronach was spared the uncomfortable optics of racing against his own conflict of interest candidate when Brian Mulroney refused to sign Steven's nomination papers. That brought local optometrist Jim Cole into the fray for the Conservatives two weeks after the campaign was officially launched. It looked to be a Stronach cakewalk to the Commons. But despite all of Magna's money and what locals recall as a very determined Liberal bid, which gave Belinda Stronach her first taste of campaign door-knocking, York–Simcoe voters sent a shocked Frank Stronach back to his boardroom in decisive defeat.

Her father remains convinced to this day that he was somehow blackballed on his application to the Commons club: "I learned a lot from it. I can't be manipulated so I don't fit into that network. If I had had the chance to speak directly to the people, I could've spoken their language and convinced them. I had no other motives but to serve society."

His ego may have been battered, but his loss came not a minute too soon for the company. Magna was in unfamiliar dire straits. Bankers were pounding at the door in 1989, threatening to call in their loan, appoint a new chairman or break up the company. Magna was hemorrhaging millions daily as the North American car market cratered, which slashed demand for parts on every make and model.

Stronach extinguished his pipe dreams for the moment and charged back to work, hell-bent on a Magna salvage mission that started at the top. He sensed the place had grown fat while he was paying attention to other things. Too many executives had two secretaries. Executive assistants were everywhere. In 1989, he closed the executive dining room, ended the free lunches for headquarters staff, eliminated company cars and cellphones for all but the most essential cases, and deflated the ballooning middle management bulge. The flowers for all reception and support staff on Secretary's Day survived, however. The trimmed-down company went back to what it did best: building car parts. It took time to restore the balance sheet to its normal gusher of black ink. The company recorded its first and, to date, only loss in 1990, a $224 million hit on the bottom line that battered a stock, which had hit $36.50 three years earlier, down to $2 a share.

IT ALL ROARED BACK in the 1990s at the dawn of an economic resurgence that sent sales of cars filled with Magna parts skyrocketing.

"In hindsight his election defeat was the best thing that could've happened, otherwise the company might not be in the same position it is today," Belinda Stronach says.

Frank Stronach promoted Don Walker to vice president of product development in 1989 who, in an unrelated by-product development, married his daughter a year later. Stronach could not have been happier. Walker is considered a genius inside and outside the company even today, a no-nonsense engineer with a sharp tactical mind who thrives on building things better and could keep Magna growing without much pan-Atlantic supervision. The bonus was having him in the clan now, linked to his daughter and seemingly set to provide him with grandchildren.

With the future of the company in solid family hands, Stronach drifted back into his worldly wandering ways. He developed a keen horse sense and pushed the company into the racetrack business in 1998 with his startling $126-million (U.S.) purchase of the venerable Santa Anita racetrack in southern California. More track acquisitions quickly followed in 1999 and 2000.

He got involved in Austrian politics, meeting with leaders and musing about starting his own party. He opened the Frank Stronach Centre of Education for Peace at Haifa University in Israel and pledged $100,000 to create a council of athletes, including gold-medal swimmer Mark Tewksbury, to act as an unofficial watchdog over the International Olympic Committee.

Sensing Canadian youth showed increasingly apathetic patriotism, he decided to motivate teenagers to dream about a better country the same way he motivated employees to work for a better Magna: cold hard cash. He set aside a million dollars in a charitable trust to spit out $20,000 for each year's winner and $10,000 for 10 finalists in an essay-writing contest. All they needed to do was complete, in roughly 2,500 words, the phrase "As Prime Minister I Would...." For Belinda Stronach, looking for a bigger challenge after 10 years on the board and a distraction from her failing first marriage, it was the perfect pet project. She tackled it with gusto, although no one had an inkling she would one day enter the competition for real.

But first things first. Someone had to inherit the overseer responsibility so that Frank Stronach had time to save the world with his ideas for individual and economic freedom for the masses. It required an attitude adjustment, but the one most like him would ultimately get the job. With his son off in his own world of tracing horse bloodlines and developing betting software, there was only one choice. In 1998, he made his daughter executive vice president of human resources. Daddy had picked his little girl to fast-track to the top.

"We are twins." It's a curious way for a father to describe a daughter, but that's the way Frank Stronach sees the relationship.

"He'll say I'm his best friend," Belinda Stronach predicts, an equally unusual claim to a father's affection. But it speaks to the central question about her motivation to succeed in business and politics: Daddy's little girl or free-thinking, independent mind? The answer would appear to be both.

She has his firm handshake, disarming eyes and easy laugh. She does not have his king-sized ego, love of being his own topic of conversation or habit of gushing forth with a random stream of consciousness on any subject. Watch them seated together and you'll witness a relaxed familiarity at play in the bemused looks they exchange while listening to others talk. Secret thoughts seem to fly between them without a word being said. The face-tightening apprehension Belinda Stronach betrays every time a camera or a tape recorder flickers to life disappears in her father's presence. She appears at ease, one of the few people allowed to stand on Frank Stronach's lofty pedestal as an equal. Indeed, perhaps she's the only one.

A promotion to vice president of human resources would be a sure sign you've climbed to the top rung of your career ladder in most corporations. The tasks surrounding severances, pensions, wrongful dismissal suits, retirement parties and union talks are far removed from the big dots on most company radars, like research, finance or product development action.

But not when you're a Stronach working at Magna International. Human relations is an epicentre of company operations. The litmus test of corporate success is keeping workers happy enough to keep the unions at bay. You get this repeated over and over again in talking to either Stronach.

"If something isn't quite fair or quite right, it will make people unhappy and unhappiness is contagious," Frank Stronach says. "If you've got unhappy people, there's no way you can make a quality product at a competitive price. We must constantly flush out the word 'unhappiness.'"

Union leaders begrudgingly admit their drives are complicated by the relative generosity of Magna's pay and profit-sharing arrangements and don't seem to hold a grudge at their multiple failed attempts. After all, former Canadian Autoworkers' Union boss Buzz Hargrove campaigned for Stronach in the 2006 election campaign.

BELINDA STRONACH insists getting interested and involved in politics was her idea and, to be fair, nobody in her circle of family or friends says differently. She felt it was thrust upon her earlier than planned, but it was an opportunity she couldn't resist. Her motivation to sacrifice a lavish lifestyle for the job of basic MP is something those close to her say is the more interesting question. There is only one explanation, according to those who have watched her in business and at home. It's a daughter out to impress a father.

He was her everything. He created the company, built the houses, bought the cars, delivered the education, provided the job and pushed the promotions. Nothing moved in her life without his say-so—until the day his "twin" stepped into the political spotlight. And it may explain why, even now where an uneventful future on the backbench beckons, she seems so insistent on sticking around. The only escape is a retreat back into her father's shadow.

"If she's successful in politics, she's beaten Frank at something," says former Magna president Jim Nicol. "Her continued success in politics is something she holds dearly because it's something that she didn't rely on him to get. Everything else in her life has been some kind of reliance either directly or indirectly on him. This is something she can say, 'I don't have to prove anything to anybody.'"

He is far from alone in this view.

"The relationship is close, but also distanced," notes second husband Johann Koss. "Belinda really wants to be herself and show that she can achieve results not because she is his daughter, but because of who she is."

BELINDA STRONACH doesn't get angry often. But any suggestion she's got a daddy-driven desire to please clearly rankles her. The smile vanishes, the green-brown eyes flash, the body language goes stiff. After many difficult hours of interviews, the first half of this exchange was the only time she openly seethed.

MARTIN: One theory that's out there is that you do [politics] partly, if not exclusively, because you've succeeded where your dad failed. Go ahead, wince away.

STRONACH: Those are people who probably don't know me. I don't feel competition with my father. I do whatever the fuck I want anyway. It's true. He probably has more respect for me for it. Growing up as a kid, my parents would often say 'Why do you have to do this'? And I'd go do it anyway. It's made me tougher in some ways. I don't see it as competition in any way. We share a passion for politics, but I'm not there to fulfill his dream, absolutely not. Case in point, I've dated a lot of guys he hasn't been happy with either, so I don't do everything he wants me to do. I can't believe when people say that....

MARTIN: I'm just baiting you.

STRONACH: I know you're baiting me, but why would I live my life to make him happy? It's important for me to be happy, to fulfill my dreams and live out my passions.

People who know me well would laugh at that comment.
I'm a very independent person. I satisfy my own soul and
my own conscience and look for what's going to give me
peace at the end of the day.

MARTIN: I see a fundamental difference between you and
him. I don't know whether he's vulnerable to ass kissers
or needs it, but you seem to look down on people who
suck up to you.

STRONACH: I don't want anyone to kiss my ass. I want people to tell me the truth. I don't harbour negative feelings
against people who give the truth to me.

MARTIN: But does your dad?

STRONACH: I wouldn't say he likes it. I'm more patient
maybe. I'm more forgiving in some ways. I take more time
to listen to people and figure out their angle. I want to
hear the truth from people and people need a comfort
level so they know they're not going to get turfed if they
say something you might not like. I don't like everything
that people say, but I ask myself if it serves the end game
better and if it does, I'm going to learn and adapt.

MARTIN: So how often do you two talk?

STRONACH: Not that often. Sometimes once a week, sometimes every two weeks. If he's in the country, he'll usually
pop in on a Sunday afternoon for tea. Mom's a little
closer. We talk once a week if I'm not in Ottawa and I'm
around. We're independent and have our own lives. It's
not like there's one person in charge of the family and
everybody drums to that beat.

MARTIN: How do you deal with, um, not sure how to say
this....

STRONACH: Go ahead, lay it out there.

MARTIN: Well, a working subtitle for this book was *Daddy's Little Girl No Longer*.

STRONACH: That's boring.

MARTIN: Yeah, it was scrapped. It's just *Belinda* now, but how do you deal with that label? Does it bug you?

STRONACH: It doesn't bug me. I'm very proud of my father in many ways. Sometimes I take him for granted a bit, but then I step back and look at what he's achieved and that he's a good man with a good heart. He's given me a unique situation and I'm appreciative of it, but he's a very strong figure and he was tough on me growing up. It wasn't Daddy's little girl. I had to fight for everything.

MARTIN: You did?

STRONACH: He comes from a very traditional background, so his thinking was that I should stay at home and raise children. I had to fight for what I wanted to do and break those barriers. So I've never felt like Daddy's little girl because I'm very independent and do exactly what I think is the right thing to do. And because it isn't a cakewalk, it's been tougher. I remember we had a conversation in my kitchen one day and I said, 'Hey I'm going to be chairman one day, I'm taking your job.' And him saying, 'You will?' Given his traditional upbringing, it would be more likely that the son would step in. I would be the good cook, although I am actually a good cook. So I had to teach him, just like your daughters are going to teach you.

MARTIN: Trust me, I'm already fully taught.

STRONACH: Good. So he's learned a lot. I don't feel it's like Daddy's little girl. It's like we're equal. I've learned from him, but I think he's learned from me as well.

There's no denying the mutual benefits from the close bond between the pair, which seems dramatically superior to the strained and perhaps obligatory connection with his son Andy. She gets the unique culture that is Frank. And in a world where everybody wants something from a billionaire with a habit of throwing money around, Frank Stronach's trust in her character and motives is uniquely and transparently powerful.

Friends still recall a flight to Europe aboard the company's Challenger jet when pilots ran into turbulence so severe, they experience it only once every 10 years. Frank Stronach was beside himself, agitating to everyone on the plane and loudly demanding the pilots get above the buffeting currents or turn back. The flight deck sent word back there was nowhere to go. Back to Gander or on to Vienna, it was going to be just as bad. Watching with alarm as their boss freaked out, staff turned to Belinda to calm her father down. As the cabin bucked and swayed in the storm, she grabbed his hand and told him to relax while the pilots searched for calmer air. Frank Stronach took a deep breath, closed his eyes and didn't say another word until the aircraft shook free of the turbulence.

"She's the only one who could've done that for him," says a friend.

SOME OBSERVERS argue Belinda Stronach is just another manifestation of the George W. Bush and Paul Martin Jr. complex. Both men were millionaires many times over and gave it all up to work in a political realm where their fathers gained fame and suffered failure. George Bush Sr. stopped short of Baghdad and taking out Saddam Hussein as U.S. president. Staid Paul Martin Sr. couldn't trump the charisma of Pierre Trudeau in his bid to become prime minister. It fell to the sons of these fathers to vindicate the family name.

In that context, consider the case of Frank Stronach. He loves to talk politics, rub elbows with national leaders and exert electoral influence through his economic clout. His only political failure was being rejected as a member of their country club when he ran as a Liberal candidate in 1988. In his daughter lay the key to the Stronach redemption.

AS HE PREPARES to take his leave of our lunch, Frank Stronach ponders a question on the most important lesson he's tried to instill in his children.

"Simple," he says finally. "Be nice to people."

You're tempted to laugh off the thought that a penniless immigrant could accrue more than $800 million, hitting the 51st spot on the 2005 *Canadian Business* rich list, without making hundreds of mortal enemies. But few in the industry or formerly of his executive suite speak harshly of Stronach. Perhaps they're afraid of his powerful global reach. "Perhaps the large severances help," confides a former executive who was a victim of the Stronach shove. Or maybe he really is nice to people.

A family friend has a clear memory of him in a New York City hotel in the early 1990s. An immigrant cleaning lady was rushing about tidying up the guest room in a hurry to get out of her VIP guests' way when Stronach stopped her and slipped a massive tip into her hand. Noting his daughter and her friend's look of surprise at his generosity, "he told us to remember that it's important to see things from the other side and never forget it," Bonnie Shore recalls. "That's rubbed off on Belinda."

"The basic philosophy of life can only be measured in the happiness you reach," Frank Stronach says with a grin while pushing back his chair to signal the interview's end and giving the serving staff a friendly farewell wave. "But it's a lot easier to be happy when you have lots of money."

FIVE

MARRIAGES, MOTHERHOOD AND MAGNA

M ARRIAGES COME and go. Motherhood is a phase. But Magna, well, that's forever. Understand that and you've grasped the essence of being a Stronach—father or daughter. The corporation may be the provider of the hedonistic Stronach lifestyle, but Magna is a family-guarded culture to be preserved for eternity against meddling by any short-sighted rulers to come. Stone tablets guarding the headquarters lobby are carved with commandments the future leaders must follow. One is nicknamed the "Magna Carta," a constitution that dictates the division of profits between shareholders, employees, research and philanthropy. The other is the Employee's Charter, which lists workers' rights to a safe, secure workplace and their freedom to snitch on bad boss behaviour using a special hotline. A controlling block of super-voting shares under Frank Stronach's sole and discretionary control fiercely protects Magna's twin pillars. You can accept them as corporate gospel or sell the stock. There is no other option. As Frank Stronach has told every journalist who has ever interviewed him, Magna operates under the golden rule: He has the gold. He rules.

ON THE EVENING of January 13, 2002, Belinda Stronach called Bonnie Shore and asked her to come over to the Aurora estate. It was unusually late, and Shore was slightly apprehensive at what could've caused her friend's sudden need for a visit. She walked into the house and spotted a bottle of champagne on ice.

"I'm going to become president of Magna tomorrow," Stronach grinned.

"Well," said Shore, "are we toasting or do we need Kleenex?"

Stronach admitted to butterflies in her stomach, but popped opened the Dom Perignon anyway. They downed a glass each and decided to call it a night. A big day was coming.

IN THE HOURS following the official announcement that presidential nepotism would replace stable, sure-footed Jim Nicol, shareholders revolted. Magna share prices experienced their biggest one-day tumble in memory, free-falling 8 percent in the opening hours of trading. After the company scrambled to assure investors that its founding chairman was still very much in hands-on control of the company and pointed to several experienced promotions in the ranks surrounding the new president, the price rebounded slightly to finish 6 percent below the day's opening.

Shareholders just didn't understand. It had to be this way. Frank Stronach insists to this day he was against his daughter's promotion to the presidency. But the board of directors clearly felt their marching orders beaming telepathically from his castle in Vienna.

"We sensed no one outside, no stranger, was going to become president if Frank wanted to move on," says Bill Davis. "We knew what Frank would like, although in fairness he did not pressure us into doing it. We were satisfied she would be a good choice."

A woman who says she "joined Magna at birth" was set to become its guardian angel. It had been in the cards for a dozen years.

THE MAGNA "CULTURE" is the result of a DNA merger between his father's Communist roots and his mother's free enterprise preference. The hybrid of socialism and capitalism created what Frank Stronach christened "fair enterprise." He has a standard Stronach Economics 101 lecture that he'll deliver at any opportunity, backed by schematic drawings with circles, squares and arrows representing the world surrounded by various conflicting forces. He will let you keep the drawing, autographed upon request, as a souvenir of getting the creator's guide to economic nirvana delivered in person.

Distilled to its most simplistic premise, fair enterprise is the belief that if all workers get a piece of the action, they'll walk through fire to make their masters more efficient, effective and, ultimately, more profitable. Greed is good for motivating the one because it benefits the corporate collective.

Stronach argues everybody longs for the same thing: freedom.

"What does individual freedom mean?" he asks. "Free to be hungry?" Nope. Freedom is really a matter of economics. "If you're not economically free, you're not a free person," he says. You press for a definition. "To put it in a simple way for Canada or the United States, it would mean that if you worked for 15 years and you lived a modest life with modest accommodation and maybe a small car, you should have saved enough to live a reasonable life off the interest. Then you could do whatever you wish with your mind, your heart, your body. This is what it's all about."

Strange, but his own father didn't buy his son's theory. Before his father died, a wealthy Stronach flew him overseas to showcase his lavish assets as proof his self-modified capitalism, not the fading force of Communism, was the answer to mankind's problems. Despite his son's obvious success, his father still "waffled" on its merits, Stronach says, shaking his head.

THE COMPANY DOESN'T attempt to hide the person who calls its shots. The founder owns special Class B shares of Stronach Trust worth 55 percent of all Magna International votes, even though they represent less than 1 percent of the issued stock.

"In addition, the Stronach Trust may, as a practical matter, be able to cause us to effect corporate transactions without the consent of our other shareholders," the company's annual report admits. "The Stronach Trust is also able to cause or prevent a change in our control."

Translation: Frank's in charge. No one can buy the company without his approval. He can sell the company without their approval. Shareholders are merely spectators, investing in his genius. That's why he can redirect an auto-parts company into racetracks, golf courses, soccer teams and art collecting. That's why he can set his own compensation package, which routinely exceeds the pay package of all five Canadian chartered bank presidents combined. And that's how he could elevate a university dropout to the level of a pharaoh on Magna's corporate pyramid in less than 10 years, a woman uniquely qualified for the one task that counts. Belinda Stronach, he knew, would defend the Magna culture as a birthright.

He named her assistant to the chairman at age 18 and gave her an office within earshot of his suite. The position hadn't existed before. Beyond answering phones and fiddling around with some junior accounting, the teenager's job description was mostly to observe, to learn and to train for her coming coronation.

Her first indoctrination into her father's world was a trip to Russia in 1987, two years before the first concrete chips were hammered off the Berlin Wall. Stronach had plans to open the Western world's first foreign-owned manufacturing plant in the Soviet Union, and needed to check out the ways of worker bees behind the Iron Curtain. The pair flew into

Moscow through Helsinki, Finland, where a Russian navigator boarded the plane. They weren't allowed to penetrate further into the Soviet Union by air. They boarded a steam train for the rest of their trip, a scene Frank Stronach recalls was straight out of *Doctor Zhivago*.

Belinda Stronach still rates the experience as a defining moment in her life, framing her behaviour as a future business leader trying to keep unions out and happy employees in. She was horrified by the working conditions after touring the Lada car factory 600 miles southeast of Moscow. It's a monster assembly line, some 22 million square feet of factory built in 1966 by 45,000 construction workers.

"It was like going back in time to the Industrial Revolution," she shudders. "They had 150,000 people in the factories. There were children and young people working there without safety equipment on muddy floors."

When guides told her top managers were paid the same as the lowest factory workers, with no prospect of any profit, never mind any sharing, Stronach couldn't figure out what made the place tick.

"There is no incentive to work," she said. "I was baffled."

BACK IN AURORA, a less traumatic travel assignment beckoned. Frank Stronach had hired art historian Denise Oleksijczuk in 1987 after a chance meeting in Venice where she was conducting art tours in a gallery. He appointed her to the idyllic task of helping him build Magna's scattered wall decorations into a world-class collection on a $500,000 annual budget. But being a political hopeful about to campaign for a Liberal seat in the 1988 election, he begged off joining her on shopping expeditions and asked Oleksijczuk if she'd give his daughter the fine arts education she wasn't getting in university.

On tours spread out over the next 18 months, the pair visited art fairs and collections in Venice, Paris, New York City and other exotic locations, buying art originals by day and sampling local cuisine by night. The chairman's daughter quickly rebelled against her father's staid artistic tastes, which gravitate toward Group of Seven paintings and wooden sculptures.

"She's really quite fearless," recalls Oleksijczuk. "I'd caution her that her purchases might be controversial and people might not like it, but she'd shrug and say 'controversy's okay.'"

If a particularly extreme work of contemporary abstract or a piece with a stiff price tag caught their eye, the two would bring it to their benefactor's attention before cutting the cheque.

"He was puzzled sometimes, but never questioned it if we both thought it was really good," recalls Oleksijczuk. "He liked these carved eagles that are sold in Colorado, which have nice optics, but are very traditional and almost knock-offs at some point because they're everywhere."

For a daughter who had trained her eye to favour old European masters, particularly the haunting works of Ireland-born expressionist Francis Bacon and Spanish master painter Francisco de Goya, wood carvings were money wasted on the mundane.

"I like artists in history who pushed the envelope and probably drove their fathers crazy," she laughs. When her father asked for her opinion on an elaborately carved eagle he fancied, she put her foot down. "Dad," she would say, "it's never going to be great art. How is it going to change anything to have another eagle on your desk? It's not going to draw a crowd."

"She pushed him to get out of his comfort zone," Oleksijczuk says.

BUT ART COLLECTING was just a brief diversion for Belinda Stronach. She was sitting on the board of directors in 1988 as the first-ever storm clouds appeared on Magna's perpetually blue horizon. The frantic pace of expansion had been financed by a billion dollars' worth of debt, and bankers picked up the scent of Magna blood as the automotive manufacturing sector hemorrhaged. With her father distracted by his more trivial pursuits, specifically that doomed run for federal political office, Stronach watched from the board above as Magna's future under family control teetered on the brink.

"Maybe he was a little less focused than he should've been," she shrugs. "But it was a very tense time. I remember the banks coming in and trying to take advantage of that debt load to break apart the company and run it. It wouldn't have been the same company today if they'd succeeded."

WITH HER FATHER'S defeat in the election, he returned to the company as a newfound disciple of debt elimination and restoring Magna to its core strengths. That meant getting rid of the playful distractions from being a car-parts business. He handed Belinda Stronach her first human resources challenge. She cloaked herself in the title of general manager and set out to serve as undertaker for one of her father's smouldering pipe dreams. He had created *Vista Magazine* in 1987 as a hip business publication for the New Age executive. And if it included stories angled toward his fair-enterprise mantra and how people could become economically free, heck, that would be just dandy too.

But for all its high-gloss looks and high-priced editorial talent, it hit the newsstands with a thud, losing millions when Magna needed every million to survive. While editors came and went through a revolving door, the magazine struggled for an identity. It was a peppy publication, brazen in places, bold in others, with enough savvy foresight to hire future Generation X icon Douglas Coupland as a cartoonist. But circulation struggled, and ad revenue limped along at a fraction of the lines in competing business publications. By the time Stronach showed up at the Toronto offices, it was obvious she was a reaper merely there to follow her father's grim order to put the publication out of its financial misery.

She tried to take the job seriously at first, listening politely to staff pouring out fresh ideas for the magazine's long-term improvement. But then she ordered the issues to become more infrequent and published on lower quality paper. She talked of moving the magazine to less spacious offices and noted there seemed to be too many staff, a problem she quickly rectified. In late 1989, with a quiet search for buyers exhausted by a void of takers, the tombstone edition of *Vista* rolled off the presses with a cover story on "How to Reshape Yourself to Recharge Your Company." The next day

Stronach stepped forward in the real role she was assigned to play—negotiating severance for the pink-slipped staff.

BACK AT MAGNA, a new and rising star was getting settled into his job as Frank Stronach's executive assistant. Don Walker had been working as a General Motors mechanical engineer when he approached Magna to discuss a joint venture in 1989. Stronach immediately spotted superior talent in the straight-shooting, six-foot-tall, athletic 31-year-old and set out to lure him to his company's managerial ranks. He had no way of knowing he was also talking to a future son-in-law. It took three offers, but Walker finally quit the car manufacturer to bring order to Stronach's increasingly chaotic office.

While planning a familiarization tour of Magna assembly plants six months into the job, Walker was approached by an attractive young blonde with a keen interest in learning the company inside out. She wondered if he'd mind some tagalong company on his travels. When it's a company director with Stronach for a last name, it's an offer you cannot refuse.

"Belinda was relatively inexperienced at business, but wanted to learn things. She's a generalist and took a broad view rather than getting into details, but she wanted to know how she could make her mark," Walker recalls.

It took only a matter of weeks before plant tours became dinner dates and dinner dates became sleepovers and that culminated in the first engagement for both, despite the fact he was 10 years her senior. The affair was kept very secret.

The notion of a key executive marrying the founder's daughter had lousy optics while Magna was in the middle of a serious restructuring to keep the bankers at bay.

The wedding—on a date the bride can no longer recall—took place at a local Anglican church with Stronach wearing a long off-white gown, followed by a lavish but small reception at her parents' new mansion on the company's sprawling Aurora estate. Across the laneway was an empty plot of land where the bride would build her next home six years later—as a divorcee. Skeptics inside the church held their tongues when the minister called for objections to the matrimonial union. The father of the bride and the maid of honour both knew what Belinda didn't at the time—it was a mismatch from the minute they'd walked down the aisle.

"I was quite happy she married him because he is one of my closest associates," recalls Frank Stronach. "I knew that it wouldn't work out in the long run, but as a father I wouldn't have tried to influence it. On one hand, you hope. But on the other hand, I knew it wouldn't work because she is a very innovative, highly intellectual person, and he is more into engineering."

Talk of the newlywed years brings back fond memories of ski trips, cottage getaways and laugh-filled dinners with friends for both Stronach and Walker, who remain trusted friends to this day. And just over a year into the marriage, they delivered news the chairman longed to hear: Frank Stronach was going to be a grandpa before his 60th birthday.

Belinda immediately decided to scale back on her Magna duties, move out of their Scarborough condo and serve as general contractor in the building of the couple's first house on Bathurst Street at King Street south of Aurora.

A month before her son's due date in November 1991, family friend Joyce Belcourt, who had met Stronach while working on her father's 1988 election campaign, stepped into the role of trainer to the mother-in-waiting. Stronach was taking a crash course in new parenting, but it was strictly by the book. Never wanting for pocket money as a teenager, Stronach had never babysat. Since her friends weren't into having children, she had yet to cuddle a baby even as one grew inside her. Belcourt decided to give her young friend's maternal instincts a jump-start by bundling her into the car and taking her to her brother's place for an afternoon of practice at holding newborn twins.

Even so, when the baby boy was born and named Frank Jr. after the ecstatic family patriarch, the new mother was traumatized.

"I don't know what to do," she moaned to her friends.

After long days and longer nights of schooling Stronach in the art of diaper-changing and baby-bathing, an exhausted Belcourt begged off and went home to her family, sending her sister-in-law Nancy Rupke to the rescue.

"When we had a kid it was like driving into a brick wall at 100 mph. This kid didn't sleep and wouldn't stop crying," Stronach recalls. "Don had a separated shoulder and so he was useless. Joyce had to stay with me for the first three days."

In November 1993, Belinda was pregnant again and daughter Nikki was born. It was the only name in the baby book the pair could agree on. By then an era of relative stability reigned in the family home. Staff members were recruited from the ranks of friends, many who remain there to this day. Rupke became her housekeeper. And high school pal Sheila Pearce signed on as her personal assistant.

TO ALL OUTSIDE appearances, things were going well in the home Stronach had built just south of Aurora as her husband's career rocketed toward Magna's pinnacle. Some Bay Street cynics figured Walker's promotions had more to do with his marriage licence than engineering degree. But inside the company, he was seen as a genius with a long-range vision of Magna expanding its car-part production into multiple-component assemblies. Eventually, he predicted, everything but the engine and drive shaft could be designed, produced and assembled off-site. It was bold and imaginative and particularly welcome as the mid-1990s approached because a restless Frank Stronach was drifting again. Among other things, he was crafting the Magna for Canada Scholarship Fund and assigning his daughter the task of running it to keep her busy.

As their fifth anniversary approached, the picture-perfect, gender-balanced happy marriage of Don and Belinda was officially an illusion. Walker was elevated to chief executive officer and was increasingly preoccupied with the job even while his wife yearned for more social activity.

"My hobby was my work in those days," he recalled.

In 1995, Stronach decided to give up any pretence of being a stay-at-home mom and returned to work as vice president of human resources. One of the first items on her to-do list was negotiate a severance—from her husband.

NEITHER SIDE WILL divulge the precise reasons for the breakup, but insist it wasn't a matter of infidelity.

"We always got along well, but we've had different views, different upbringings and different values in a few areas," Walker allows. "But we figured we wanted to keep a strong relationship because of our children."

The pair finally called a matrimonial summit to discuss the state of their souring union and asked themselves an honest question: "Were we 100 percent motivated to stay in the relationship long term? I think the answer was no," says Walker. "It wasn't a big blow-up with a big fight or anything. It was just a mutual decision and probably the most stress-free breakup you could have. We just sat down over the course of an evening and did up the separation. Lawyers were never involved."

Frank and Elfriede Stronach, despite being in a love-challenged marriage of their own, were mortified when their daughter announced she was leaving her husband. They begged her to stick it out for the sake of the children, not to mention preserving the peace at Magna. A divorce between the chief executive officer and the founder's daughter was potentially even more complicated for the company than their marriage.

Belinda Stronach would not be deterred. A friendly separation with joint custody was better than an empty marriage for all concerned, she argued.

"Life is too short if you don't get along with people," Stronach says. "If you're unhappy, why are you unhappy? You have to address that in a very logical way."

Walker moved out and she started planning to build her dream home just a couple hundred metres away from her parents' front door.

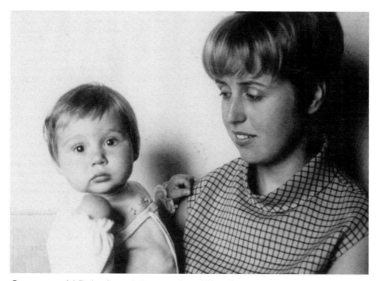

One-year-old Belinda with her mother, Elfriede.

Belinda (right) delivers her long wish list to Santa, while baby brother Andy struggles to escape St. Nick's knee.

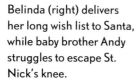

Her shy phase was ending as Belinda Stronach prepared to enter high school the same year her father's Magna International became a billion-dollar company. Here the 12-year-old (fourth from right, middle row) is pictured with her Grade Eight class from Rogers Public School in Aurora, Ontario.

Belinda poses on her 16th birthday with the silver Z/28 Indy 500 pace car given to her by her parents.

Left to right: Cocktails with high school pals Lori Lemieux, Carol Loschke and Sheila Pearce.

Left to right: Magna executive Al Power, six-time World Champion extreme speed skier Franz Weber, Belinda, 1970s World Cup runner-up Klaus Heidegger and friend Carl Reider pose before hitting the slopes at Island Lake Lodge in Fernie, BC.

Sheila Pearce and Belinda ham it up after buying earmuffs during a shopping expedition in Melbourne, Australia.

Belinda Stronach weds first
husband, Donald Walker, in an
Aurora church in 1990.
(Al Gilbert, C.M.)

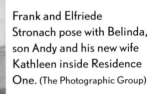

Frank and Elfriede
Stronach pose with Belinda,
son Andy and his new wife
Kathleen inside Residence
One. (The Photographic Group)

Belinda and second husband, Johann Koss, arrive at their New Year's Eve 1999 wedding reception in Colorado. (Warwick Brown Fine Photography, warwickbrown.com)

Frank Stronach at his daughter's second wedding. (Warwick Brown Fine Photography, warwickbrown.com)

Belinda poses with Johann outside the Coliseum in Rome, Italy.

Belinda Stronach meets Bill Clinton for the first time while he participated in a Toronto Sick Children's Hospital fundraiser at Frank Stronach's invitation. (© Peter Redman/*National Post*)

Friend, celebrity stylist and judge on *Canada's Next Top Model*, Paul Venoit (left), with U2 front man, Bono, and his pal Belinda.

Stronach crosses party lines when it comes to hanging around with former Ontario premiers. Left to right: Conservative Mike Harris, Conservative Bill Davis and Liberal David Peterson all call her friend. Peterson would play a key role in negotiating her defection to the Liberals. (Warwick Brown Fine Photography, warwickbrown.com)

In happier days when she was a Conservative, Stronach was a regular in the lofty social orbit of Brian and Mila Mulroney. (Tom Sandler)

Stronach receiving an honourary doctorate from McMaster University president Peter George on June 3, 2003. (Robert Tatlock, McMaster University)

Magna hits the New York Stock Exchange on October 9, 2002. Company president Belinda Stronach rings the opening bell. To her right is Canada's Consul General to New York, former broadcaster and journalist Pamela Wallin. (Warwick Brown Fine Photography, warwickbrown.com)

"Their personalities are very different," explains Pearce. "If you spend a couple of hours with them, you'd never imagine how they could be married. Both are great people, but very different, and they weren't happy together and recognized that."

AFTER THE AMICABLE divorce, Stronach went walkabout. Her children were entering school, so the demands on her time at home eased. Her Magna position was somewhat awkward because she reported to her former husband, who was still under the direct control of her father. She bought into Misura, a fashion label under award-winning designer Joeffer Caoc, and began regular commutes to Saks Fifth Avenue and other New York fashion houses, promoting the designs and modelling the merchandise on every social occasion, which were becoming more and more frequent. She also dived into the Magna Scholarship fund, sifting through stacks of essays to pick the winners and hand out the cheques.

If Belinda needed a jolt to reignite her zeal for life, it came with an infamous death during the dog days of summer 1999. John F. Kennedy Jr., then 38, came calling on Stronach to size her up as a potential investor in his money-losing magazine. *George* had an irreverent and witty take on politics, but hadn't made a nickel of profit after four years on the stand. The son of the late U.S. president was getting low on sources to tap for cash. New York writer Leslie Marshall said her pal Belinda Stronach had deep pockets and a creative imagination. She just might find a magazine with a high readership among upscale women appealing. It was music to JFK Jr.'s ears.

On Monday, July 12, 1999, he flew into Toronto's Buttonville airport piloting his single-engine plane with his broken ankle in a cast. The two, along with Marshall and Magna executive Keith Stein, sat on the patio of her new residence and talked politics, personalities and the magazine market Kennedy was trying to reach. Stronach said she was interested and would explore the possibility of Magna making an investment.

Before they parted, Kennedy offered Marshall a lift back to New York on his plane. But Stein had a strange ominous feeling about the offer and strongly insisted she return aboard a commercial flight instead. Marshall agreed and Kennedy shrugged. The luncheon broke up with hugs and promises to keep in touch.

Four days later Kennedy, freed from his cast and no longer requiring a co-pilot to operate the foot pedals, disappeared into a dark haze hanging over Martha's Vineyard on a moonless night and vanished from New York radar screens. Investigations later concluded that a lost and disoriented Kennedy inadvertently flew his plane into the ocean, killing his wife and sister-in-law.

Stronach was at the family cottage when CNN flashed word that Kennedy's plane had disappeared. He had visited Canada only a few days earlier, the story noted.

"After that I became determined to get the most out of every day," Stronach says. "Here was this guy just coming into his own. He was intelligent, handsome, smart, developing self-confidence and had a platform for his interests. He gets on a plane and has no idea what is about to happen. He's sitting out there on my patio on a Monday and dies on a Friday. I learned you can't wait for everything to be perfect."

Later that year, she lobbied for a better title and was appointed executive vice president of Magna's human resources. Still, she wanted more. She can remember driving along a highway in Austria with Siegfried Wolf, then head of Magna's European operations. He was reciting a list of acquisitions, company revamps and assorted challenges he was facing. Stronach was transfixed by the notion of having a hands-on impact on changing company operations for the better. Suddenly, the goal of becoming the ceremonial overseer of Magna as the board chair seemed less attractive than it had been as a teenager.

"Being CEO had seemed so ambitious," Stronach says. "But after hearing Ziggy, I decided, 'Shit, the only way I can get involved in changes is as CEO.'"

One small problem. The job was held by her former husband.

BEFORE ELBOWING into the top slot, Stronach would enter the rarified ranks of international sports superstardom. It wasn't entirely a question of superior athletics. She would do it the hard way—by marrying one.

One of her father's more dramatic departures from the auto-parts business was to challenge the tainted Olympic Games bidding process. Throughout the 1980s and 1990s, landing host-city rights became more about the best bribes than the best bids. Whenever International Olympic

Committee members paid a visit to a hopeful host, they were treated with red-carpet reverence and sometimes a monetary gift or two. Such misbehaviour peaked in the ugly swirl of IOC vote-buying allegations surrounding the successful Salt Lake City bid for the 2002 Games.

In the late-1990s, Frank Stronach donated $100,000 to create the awkwardly named Olympic Advocates Together Honourably (OATH), led by multiple gold-medal swimmer Mark Tewksbury and chaired by his daughter along with her close friend George Marsland. It went way over budget as the group attempted to shine a spotlight of embarrassing publicity on the so-called Lords of the Rings, forcing them to clean up their act. They were instantly dismissed as a "belly flop" by IOC brass after they tried to crash a meeting at IOC headquarters in Lausanne, Switzerland. In this volunteer role, Stronach took a trip to England in early 1999 where family friend Keith Stein, with a twinkle in his eye, arranged a meeting with a Norwegian speed skater he bumped into a few months earlier in Japan. When Belinda Stronach was introduced to Johann Olav Koss, it was passion at first sight.

While speed-skating champions supernova into North American superstars every four years during the 16 days of Winter Games competition, they are perennial celebrities in Scandinavian countries. In Norway, he's media sensation King Koss, a title the modest medical doctor abhors. But when it came to speed skating, Koss did indeed rule the ovals in the early 1990s.

He was officially launched into orbit at the 1992 Albertville Olympics, emerging from two days in hospital for a pancreatic ailment to grab a gold and silver medal in the

1,500 and 10,000 events respectively. With the IOC's switch to alternating summer and winter Olympiads, Koss was handed another golden opportunity just two years later at Norway's Lillehammer Games. With the euphoric crowd behind their hometown hero, Koss swept a trio of gold medals to claim Sportsman of the Year honours in *Sports Illustrated* magazine. Later that year he set three world records en route to winning his third All-Round World Championship in the sport.

But between his two turns in Olympic competition, Koss visited the poverty-stricken Ethiopian breakaway country of Eritrea as part of the Olympic Aid program, a humanitarian fund set up to assist the war-ravaged 1984 host city of Sarajevo. Watching pre-teen children playing soccer with rolled up shirts on dirt patches obstructed by partially destroyed tanks, Koss had an epiphany of sorts. He resolved to use his celebrity status to raise money so the children of oppressed countries were given a chance, if not the right, to play sports.

The next year, bathed in the media spotlight for his gold-medal haul, he used the microphones to push his agenda to help the kids of Africa win the right to play sports. The money poured in—some $18 million that year—and he donated his Games winnings to the cause before starting his own organization called Right to Play. For his humanitarian efforts, Koss was crowned one of *Time Magazine*'s "100 Future Leaders of Tomorrow" and by the World Economic Forum as "One of 1,000 Global Leaders."

Ironically, his imminent wife would be named one of the top 80 global leaders by the same Forum just six years later.

Sparks flew at first blush between Stronach and Koss, who is two years her junior, during and after their London introduction. Things went pan-Pacific when she visited him in Australia later that year, where he was finishing medical school. He found her incredibly attractive, yet fascinating as a woman born rich with a deep social conscience.

"A quote she uses a lot is about the redistribution of wealth and how it is divided between the poor and the rich," Koss says now. "That's kind of interesting coming from a person who has a very affluent background, but who also has a sense of responsibility to give back to individuals who don't have as much."

Stronach was amazed by the fact Koss could summon senior United Nations officials with the flick of his cellphone and dazzled by his global reputation as an advocate for the most disadvantaged. But, as her drooling friends noted, the guy also had the chiselled good looks and muscular body of a Norwegian god, and worked hard at keeping it that way. There was a lot of serious heat in their relationship, they say.

MERE MONTHS INTO their globetrotting romance, Koss went down on bended knee atop a mock Eiffel Tower in a Las Vegas casino and proposed. Stronach didn't hesitate for a second to say yes, hoping this do-over marriage was for keeps. They decided to risk an infestation of Y2K bugs and set the wedding date for New Year's Eve 1999. It was an intimate affair with only 40 invited guests and was held at a stone chapel just down the mountain from The Château, the family's Beaver Creek ski home and condominium complex. Larger receptions followed in Oslo and Toronto a month later. The Norwegian press was in a frenzy to get the low-down on their sports king's first queen. They demanded pictures and Koss complied, sending off eye-popping photos of Stronach in her Joeffer Caoc–designed silver-blue strapless dress wrapped in a midnight blue faux fur coat.

Yet even while the traditional Norwegian fanfare of trumpets started the ceremony, there were skeptics in the audience. The same maid of honour and the same father of the bride from the first wedding had fresh doubts.

"It happened way too quickly," shrugs Sheila Pearce. "I recognized it at the time, but you can't say anything to some-one when they're completely in love."

Koss received a hero's welcome when he returned home to Norway that year, bringing Stronach and her children to meet his family before hiking high into the fjords. The couple moved into Stronach's new mansion in the family compound, and she went back to work as executive vice president of human resources. He set out to convince the world to join his crusade to give kids in slums a reason to live through sports activity.

"In some ways we had an incredibly interesting time together, and I hope I opened her eyes to the world outside of Canada," Koss says now.

When the newlyweds visited Africa in 2001 and stumbled upon a lineup of 3,000 Ghana women with children waiting for malaria shots, Koss says the scene clearly hit his spouse hard: "It was obvious that it touched Belinda that these women travelled from distant places with nothing, just to try and save their children through a vaccination program."

He got a sneak preview of his wife's growing political interest when, less than a month into their marriage, she dragged him to Ottawa for the Think Big founding convention of the Canadian Alliance. As president of an organization that fends off political involvement with a barge pole, Koss took one look at the Rideau Canal, frozen every winter into the longest skating rink in the world, and did what comes naturally to him—he spent the day speed-skating while the politicians talked.

But it was an unsustainable frantic pairing between individuals spending too many weeks apart and too little time together. His drive for perfection physically and the intensity of a non-stop lifestyle requiring only four hours sleep a night soon overwhelmed the relationship.

"It came very quickly together, and I realized we were basically also very different. We can continue to be good friends, but the partnership doesn't work out because our expectations are different than what each of us could fulfill," says Koss.

Less than two years into the marriage, Stronach was seen hitting the party circuit solo, and gossips spotted her guzzling champagne in the bars and Brazilian balls in Toronto with other men. Also complicating things were fresh sightings and frenzied press coverage of Stronach with no ordinary Bill. The tabloid press had pictures of her giving former U.S. President Bill Clinton an adoring look at a golf course. She was instantly dubbed "Bubba's babe."

And then, suddenly, it was over. He moved to downtown Toronto. She stayed in Aurora.

"It was exciting and passionate, but they shouldn't have gotten married. It should've been a two-year relationship, and then they could've moved on," says Pearce.

A prenuptial agreement came into force to deny Koss a serious slice of the Magna fortune in the event of divorce, but one close friend says he didn't leave entirely empty-handed. There's a lingering sense their breakup was less amicable than the Walker divorce, but a dome of silence covers all disclosures. This much is known though: The couple still talk periodically and Koss remains a devoted stepfather to Stronach's children.

HER GOLDEN MOMENT of opportunity finally arrived in February 2001. Chief executive officer Don Walker wasn't content as Magna spun off into five self-operating divisions, leaving headquarters disconnected from autonomous plant operations. He's a hands-on engineer who wanted to be in charge of manufacturing a product. Reading balance sheets from afar and herding the operating-division cats in the same general direction wasn't his idea of fun. When the presidency of auto-interior spinoff Inteir opened up, Walker decided to grab it. The CEO position became conveniently vacant; no outsider needed to apply. The short list was already in the hands of directors. And it had only one name. Belinda.

"You ask what excites me and it is the Magna Constitution," she gushes even now. "I still don't know of other companies that have a system that defines how you split up profits and can't be changed by any CEO." That's the sort of attitude that, on January 14, 2002, put a 35-year-old into the CEO suite of a $10.5 billion company employing 62,000 staff with offices and factories in 18 countries.

Her father ensured Stronach wasn't left unsupervised, however, keeping president Jim Nicol nearby and proven auto industry managers watching her back as vice presidents. The board of directors of the time was a veritable Who's Who of old-time politicians, including former Ontario Tory premiers Bill Davis and Mike Harris, former Cabinet ministers Ed Lumley and Doug Young, and former Liberal MP Dennis Mills, who had served as parliamentary secretary to the minister of Industry. And because Magna had been decentralized into stand-alone subsidiaries, each with its own independent management structure, board and corporate headquarters, Stronach seemed to be a CEO-Lite, put in charge of little more than investor, supplier and employee relations. The tricky part, she says, was to avoid being seen as merely the front for her father, who dominated public events whenever Magna was in the spotlight, and didn't seem reluctant to shove his daughter into the shadows.

"It was important not to be seen as spy or the pipeline to my father, so I really worked hard to get [the] trust and respect of my co-workers," says Stronach.

Her ability to connect with the shop floor, talking to workers and managers with equal dexterity, was considered a valuable asset when stacked up against a standoffish board and executive ranks. She is very much her father's daughter in the sense of being approachable and having no fear of surrounding herself with the brightest lights she could find. But her father notes a fundamental difference in their managerial styles.

"I've always been more direct," says Frank Stronach. "Because she's a female, she's a little more diplomatic and a little more refined. I come on like a bulldozer for the simple reason I'm a driven person. I want to be number one in the world. I haven't got time for nice flowers. I tried to be cultivated and I don't want to insult anybody unless it was necessary."

Don Walker agrees.

"In personality and the way they analyze things, there's a lot of similarities between and Frank and Belinda," he says. "In execution, in how they deal with people, I would say they're quite different. She'd be more of a consensus builder, a team builder, while Frank would look at something and say, 'Let's just get it done.'"

But there wasn't much to get done under her watch, at least in terms of aggressive intervention in the affairs of satellite operations. Magna managers view their plants as their own, and ask only to be left alone so they can work toward securing their share of boosted profits. As captain of the mother ship circling in the distance, Stronach's role became less about building a better truck-door assembly and more about seeking expansion opportunities while ensuring employees were pampered enough to deter CAW leader Buzz Hargrove from successful union-certification drives.

"She was a very good CEO. Magna was the kind of organization where a lot of it was run by plant managers and individuals in charge of various sections," agrees former director Bill Davis. "Belinda's great strength was her ability to bring the two or three principals doing the day-to-day operations together to achieve a consensus. She had great abilities in keeping people focused and ultimately singing from the same hymnal. In a company like Magna, that was not an insignificant accomplishment."

With her new stature, she became the standout blonde in a sea of blue-suited automotive heavyweights. It had its awkward moments. A classic case was a pivotal meeting of Ford executives in Detroit in 2001. Senior executives moved in when Stronach, dressed to kill, entered the room escorted by a junior male official.

"Who," wondered one Ford executive to the young man patronizingly, "is this lovely lady?"

Stronach interrupted the conversation to introduce herself as Magna CEO and her junior executive as, well, her junior executive.

"That's why I never attend a meeting carrying a purse," she smirks.

Stronach began collecting blue-chip add-ons to her resumé to bolster her credentials as Magna's glamour boss. She was suddenly listed as a member of the Dean's Council at the prestigious John F. Kennedy School of Government at Harvard University. Her $5-million donation to the school was spun as purely coincidental. She was named to the dean's advisory board of the University of Toronto's Rotman School of Management the same year Magna made a million-dollar donation to create a chair at the university. It was heady stuff for a B-average high school student and first-year university dropout. Where there's a will, one argues, money will find a way.

She also became a fixture at international think tanks, usually bringing along then husband Johann Koss for additional star wattage. She was a regular (although a somewhat irregular guest being a woman) at the secretive Davos gathering in Switzerland, and ensured she was always on the guest list at the annual World Economic Forum. It wasn't all just schmoozing with world leaders and deep thinkers, though. While at the 2002 World Economic Forum, Stronach became alarmed at the sudden drop in Canada's competitiveness ranking. It had been third the year earlier. Now it was eighth. She convened an intimate breakfast with Canadian journalists, politicians, academics and business leaders and summoned the Forum's chief economist to explain the criteria for the ranking's free fall. Among the invitees was Jim Flaherty, now federal finance minister, who angrily pooh-poohed the process.

ON JANUARY 14, 2002—almost exactly two years to the day before she would give it up—Belinda Stronach got it all. With Nicol's abrupt departure to join Tomkins PLC in Britain, she was promoted to the presidency and had her former chief executive officer title abolished. As mentioned earlier, the stock market was not impressed. It voted in a burst of panic selling.

"There's no question that her ability to get to the top of that organization was because she was the boss's daughter," recalls Nicol now. "When it came to protecting the Magna culture, there'd be no one better positioned than Belinda in the company."

Former co-workers consistently credit Stronach with an ability to learn quickly, even if advanced international business theories don't pour off her tongue. She also has an intuitive sense of people, and can instantly separate those with something to offer her from those who are out to get something from her.

While orbited by competent managers and supervised by Frank Stronach from Vienna, her presidency would prove soothingly uneventful, even while she posted strong results on the balance sheet. Insiders say she brought much-needed stability to the company's somewhat erratic deviations from the automotive-parts business under her father's hand. As more than one executive noted, Stronach made headquarters a fun place to work again. That was partly because she buffered company brass from her father's whimsical and sometimes unjustifiable personnel changes. And, senior executives recall, there was considerable value in having someone at the top who could veto her father's brainstorms without becoming instant collateral damage.

"On some big issues she'd say no, but she always did it in the right way. Belinda had great sense of not taking Frank on and embarrassing him in front of a crowd," remembers Nicol. "She knew there was no sense in embarrassing anybody because people have a sense of self-worth."

STRONACH DID PILOT the spinoff of Magna Entertainment Corp. into its own entity, and continued to acquire small and medium-sized enterprises whenever the opportunity arose. She talks of having been an early Magna proponent of moving toward China as a manufacturing opportunity and untapped market, a claim others confide is exaggerated. Beyond that, news coverage of her two-year presidency is slim and almost exclusively about her social activities and globetrotting trips to international symposiums.

Directors struggled to recall a signature move by Belinda Stronach as president.

"I can't say she was involved in any particular acquisition, but she did bring a degree of stability," insists Davis. "She was there. Now if you want to infer that Frank wasn't always there, he would say that to you. Her task was not to be, shall we say, as creative as her father in terms of new things to be doing," he adds. "She concentrated on making what was there work. Frank not only did that, but he was creating areas of new interest like [Magna Entertainment] and so on."

Her caretaker role may have been reflected in her compensation envelope, which was barely a tenth of the $30- to $50-million haul that accrued to her father every year. Stronach insists she was offered large raises and rejected them: "I wanted to establish my reputation first."

Going strictly by the numbers, she clearly succeeded. Magna's financial results exceeded expectations on every count. While she held the presidency, the company delivered a three-year shareholder return of 41.4 percent, a five-year increase in net income of 116 percent and profit increases, despite declines in vehicle production in North America and Europe. The share price peaked during her reign and, as of this writing, has yet to be matched.

"A lot of people say she was only there because of Frank. She was there because of Frank, no question, but she also performed," notes Davis.

Don Walker, who has since returned to Magna as co-CEO under more difficult times with commodity prices rising and domestic manufacturers in dire straits, gives a modest tip of the hat to his former wife when it is pointed out her stock market track record beats his handily.

"Part of it is cyclical," says Walker, "but the company did well while Belinda was here, partly for what she was doing, partly because it is what was happening in the industry and partly what was happening in the operating companies that were consolidated in Magna."

But if her performance was more about being a lucky puppet than a shrewd business leader, the global media were clearly duped. *Fortune* magazine ranked her number 2 in a list of the world's most powerful women in business. The World Economic Forum named her one of its 80 global leaders of tomorrow. Honours poured in, including Canadian Women Executive of the Year, which had her wondering why women were relegated to a special gender classification.

And in early 2004, Belinda Stronach hit the headiest times of all when *Time Magazine* anointed her one of the world's 100 Most Influential People. She had finally jumped ahead of her father onto the world stage. It wasn't going to get any better than that for a Canadian heiress with a party-girl reputation and no university degree. It seemed like the right time for her short attention span to kick in. The boardroom was getting boring. And besides, an unexpected window of political opportunity was opening wide.

SIX

THE MOUNTAIN
AWAITS

B ELINDA STRONACH'S flirtation with politics started in
1988 when she watched her father run and lose in the
Newmarket riding for the federal Liberals, an unlikely
pairing between a global business leader and a party hell-bent
on killing the North American Free Trade Agreement. She'd
door-knocked for Frank Stronach, folded his "Frankly
Speaking" pamphlets and answered phones at his campaign
office. But her interest was clearly oriented toward the various manifestations of the Conservative Party.

She'd met Reform Party Leader Preston Manning as a
young mother in the early 1990s.

"She went out of her way to meet Preston," former campaign
worker Jack Hurst told *Toronto Life* magazine in June 2004. "She
brought over little Frank Jr., who was still in a carriage."

Stronach's attraction to the right wing of the political
spectrum had more to do with Manning than the Reform

Party. While she was a social moderate—pro-choice and in favour of expanded gay rights right from the beginning—Manning's ideas for democratic reform, such as the use of referendum, MP recall and fixed election dates, were particularly appealing to her, an interest that would surface later in her political life.

She attended the United Alternative conference, which led to the creation of the Canadian Alliance, and dived into the revamped party's leadership race by supporting Tom Long's bid before throwing her clout behind Manning, who thanked her for her "unflagging support" of the Reform Party and the Canadian Alliance in his memoirs.

Then a boyish former Crown prosecutor from Nova Scotia had caught her eye politically, if not yet personally, as the 2003 race to replace Joe Clark in the Progressive Conservative leadership got under way. She eventually raised $250,000 for MP Peter MacKay's campaign, but found the Bay Street crowd increasingly stingy about opening their vaults to fund two conservative parties beating each other up at the polls during every federal election.

"A number of us were leading the charge to get this party together. We told them, 'We're no longer interested in helping either one of you perpetuate two parties,'" Mike Harris recalls. "Belinda became engaged in that process. I was into some pretty serious fundraising and the money people I knew said, 'Go away, we're not giving you any more. You guys can duke it out separately for the next 50 years for all we care.'"

It may or may not have been Stronach's idea—others suggest she was merely the front for a greater backroom effort by political titans like Harris, former Ontario Premier Bill

Davis, former Deputy Prime Minister Don Mazankowski and former Prime Minister Brian Mulroney—but she had phoned then leader of the Canadian Alliance Party Stephen Harper in the weeks following MacKay's victory to see if he'd agree to preliminary merger talks.

The pair met at the Official Opposition leader's Ottawa residence in mid-June 2003, where Stronach raised the idea of appointing two or three emissaries from each party to secretly explore reunification talks far from the media spotlight. Harper said it made sense to him and green-lighted the scheme. Stronach flew to Montreal to meet MacKay and proposed the same thing and got the same answer. She recalls the trio meeting for lunch on a sunny summer day at Magna's Simeone House, where both sides agreed to quietly kick-start the reunification effort as the leaders stayed aloof from the fray.

"I would describe her as a key facilitator. She played a very large role in getting them off the dime," says Mulroney. "Once they got going, then it was up to the leaders."

"It's fair to state that she did play a role in persuading the two principals not to abandon the process and that was not an unimportant role," says former Ontario Premier Bill Davis, one of the negotiators at the table. "More so with Harper than MacKay, she was encouraging him or persuading him not to abandon the process."

With Stronach's encouragement, Harper chased MacKay around southern Ontario to keep negotiations from breaking down over the leadership voting process. MacKay correctly figured the larger Alliance would swallow the Progressive Conservatives and demanded every riding be given equal weight in the vote. When Harper agreed to his terms, a log-jam broke and the reunification went forward. Still, even future nemesis Harper tipped his hat to Stronach after party members approved the merger in the fall of 2003.

"She was overwhelmingly concerned about the lack of competition at the federal level and wanting to see a real choice in Canadian democracy," Harper allowed. "She put quite a few hours into this and, with her clock running, those were pretty expensive hours."

What Harper did not know at the time was that a lack of competition for the federal party's leadership would ulti-mately bring Belinda Stronach into the political spotlight—*his* political spotlight.

STRONACH'S RISE to prominence on the Canadian political scene was so sudden and meteoric, her star-is-born moment can be traced to a specific morning: October 17, 2003. That's when news broke that she'd been a key behind-the-scenes player in the merger talks. It seemed an obvious plant, per-haps the result of her recent hire of image-maker Bonnie Brown, former aide to Mila Mulroney. The rumour mill wasn't far behind in churning out speculation she would seek the leadership. Stronach insists she didn't covet the job initially. Friends and associates, apparently acting on her request, fanned out to kill the speculation.

"Dead, dead, dead," Toronto Liberal MP Dennis Mills, a family friend, insisted to reporters when asked about her leadership ambitions. Stronach herself hit the phones to deny interest in entering politics.

"I have no intention of seeking the leadership of the new party. I remain fully committed to my corporate responsibilities at Magna and my family," she said.

Besides, there were already several hefty names in active speculation with solid track records backed by large ready-to-roll organizations. Former Ontario Premier Mike Harris. New Brunswick Premier Bernard Lord. Alberta Premier Ralph Klein. And, of course, merger-displaced leaders Stephen Harper and Peter MacKay.

As the weeks went by, Stronach became increasingly worried the reunification effort would culminate in a second-verse-same-as-the-first result with barely a fight. Harper had a hammerlock on the much larger Alliance organization and its membership, which gave him control of most ridings in the West and rural Ontario. A draft-Harris movement had begun taking shape in Ontario and Alberta, but the former premier quickly pulled himself out of the race. Klein was never a serious contender, and Jim Prentice entered the race only to quickly withdraw. Stronach was also being told privately that MacKay had extreme doubts about running, having barely recovered personally and financially from his PC leadership race.

With only former Ontario Health Minister Tony Clement and a possible bid by Lord to seriously challenge Harper, seeking the leadership herself occurred to Stronach.

"Too much effort was put into the merger only to have Stephen Harper win it again," she says now. "I'd always had an interest in running at some point in my life. If Peter [MacKay] would've run, I wouldn't have run. The timing wasn't ideal, but others wouldn't step forward and it needed different viewpoints."

In early November 2003, Belinda Stronach pulled her father aside after a Magna board meeting at the golf club and told him she was toying with the idea of seeking the reunited Conservative leadership.

"He said, 'I'll support you and I'll get back into Magna, but it's a big hill to climb,'" she recalls him saying.

A group of friends and family called a pre-winter huddle in the Stronach family's Florida mansion to discuss the idea. Some flagged the galling notion of a business executive leaping straight into a federal party leadership without political experience as a fatal handicap. Others argued she could become the next Brian Mulroney, who turned his outsider status into the largest government majority in Canadian history. Stronach took a ski getaway to Aspen and hit the biggest bumps on the slipperiest slopes she could find to think about it—a fitting metaphor for the consequences of her decision. She was haunted by an image that dominates much of her thinking at every personal crossroads—that of being 80 years old and looking back on her life with regret at having given life-altering challenges a pass.

This, she decided, was precisely the sort of opportunity that deserved to be seized.

I joined Mike Harris as one of Ralph Klein's roasters at a Calgary homeless shelter fundraiser on November 12, 2003. The former Ontario premier and Magna board member had bowed out of the contest a few days earlier, but listened patiently to my commiseration at the thin slate of hopefuls that seemed to foreshadow a Harper coronation instead of a much-needed contest.

"Relax," he said. "There is another."

I was perplexed. All the usual suspects, including Stronach, had declared themselves disinterested or disinclined.

"Wait and see," he grinned as I went through a list of far-fetched contenders, shaking his head. "The race isn't over yet."

Just days earlier he'd talked to Stronach about what lay ahead as she weighed the pros and many cons of leaving the private family cocoon for life under an intense public microscope.

"I told her what this life was going to be like, that her private life would be completely exposed," Harris says. "Was she ready for that? Both of us [Harris, along with Bill Davis, both Magna directors at different times] gave her lots of cautions. I thought she would be a long shot to win, but felt it would be tremendous for the party to have her there. It was better for the party than it was for Belinda, frankly, but it might be good for her in the long run too. She could bring something to the party, and if her goal was to one day be prime minister, that was achievable."

But Harris knew his friend was starting very, very late in the game. Having only three months to take a political neophyte from the boardroom to the big leagues of a federal party leadership was going to require miracle workers. He got out his Rolodex and started rounding up the brightest members of his scattered team. Harris also plotted an "accidental" encounter between his candidate and the most experienced campaign organizer in the business.

John Laschinger runs his star-making operation from a cramped office on Bay Street in downtown Toronto as an associate of Northstar Research Partners. His desk is buried under teetering stacks of paper and files. The walls feature articles about the candidates, winners and more than a few losers that he's backed at various political levels with varying party affiliations.

Laschinger was between campaigns in late 2003, but feeling upbeat as he waited for a potential client to green-light his bid for the Conservative Party leadership. Bernard Lord had lit oratorical fire during a keynote speech at the party's founding convention to euphoric reviews from the crowd and media observers. He was instantly catapulted to the rank of serious contender and became the subject of an intense draft as he pondered the big leap forward. It was a giddy prospect, and Laschinger was looking forward to the challenge of backing Lord the night he attended the annual Harris Christmas party at the former premier's residence.

With the booze flowing and the party starting to wind down, Belinda Stronach arrived to work the room and bumped into Laschinger, by design if not accident. Small talk ensued before Laschinger asked if the rumours of her interest in the Conservative leadership were true. Yes, she said, the leadership was an intriguing idea. Would he be available to help if she entered the race? Laschinger shrugged. Sorry. He was booked to do the Lord's work.

The next day, Magna executive Keith Stein called to ask Laschinger out for coffee. A hyper-energetic type A personality who can eat six meals a day without adding an ounce to his toothpick frame, Stein is viewed by Magna employees as having a ruthless, take-no-prisoners loyalty to the family as

Frank Stronach's henchman and Belinda Stronach's corporate guardian. Stein didn't mince words when the pair met at a local Starbucks. What are Stronach's negatives? Would he help? When could he sign on? Laschinger, a grizzled, unflappable burly bear of a man, looked at Stein like he just didn't get it. Bernard Lord was his client, and helping Stronach was at cross-purposes to that loyalty. A strategist can't serve two masters in a single race, he said. Stein left disappointed.

His disappointment didn't last long. Lord bowed out a week later, citing family commitments and the fact he held but a single seat cushion of majority comfort in his New Brunswick legislature. Laschinger sighed. Bilingual with a track record of provincial accomplishment and national name recognition, Lord would've been an easier sell, but at least money would never be a problem on the Stronach campaign. He ordered up a poll of Conservative members to scope the chances of taking a rich blonde from big business to political centre stage with just over two months remaining in the rush to sell voting memberships. The polling came back with the odds.

"Shitty," he recalls in hindsight. Stronach was very much an unknown in party circles and only 7 percent of members surveyed supported her candidacy.

On January 7, 2004, Stronach called Laschinger to request a face-to-face meeting. Two days later, she showed up in the Northstar boardroom to receive a skeptical welcome from the man she wanted to guide her campaign.

"Look," she said, "for the last month people have been telling me how high the mountain is. I want you to tell me how to climb it."

Laschinger cursed his lousy luck. He had a candidate with desire and the money, but no serious qualifications for the job. He'd lost a candidate with the qualifications to win and no mountain-climbing desire. He opted to give it to her straight. It was going to be hell. The media would be merciless. He warned her she probably couldn't win and she should have no designs on becoming prime minister. That, Laschinger figured, would send his potential client whimpering back to the Magna compound. He was surprised when Stronach stood up, extended her hand for a shake and told him to unleash her campaign.

"The mountain awaits," she grinned.

Laschinger commissioned a more detailed round of polling, trying to see a glimmer of hope to motivate his 45th campaign. It took a vivid imagination. Most of those polled favoured the merger, but they thought it would take two elections to place the government under the new party's banner. Three-quarters believed a business background was a positive and embraced a middle-of-the-road philosophy. A slim majority had heard of Stronach, but only 16 percent had a favourable impression. Most didn't know if she was right or left on the political spectrum. Of those surveyed, Laschinger found 55 percent would vote for Stephen Harper right then and there. He felt that support was rock solid (three months later, Harper won with 55.5 percent of the vote). The only hope for Stronach was to expand the moderate membership base dramatically and quickly. And that meant campaigning against Prime Minister Paul Martin, not Stephen Harper.

It was thin gruel and Laschinger knew it. There might be no way to win, but if Stronach stayed safely inside his bubble and didn't fall through the many trap doors set to spring by the salivating horde of media, there was a chance to save his candidate from personal and political humiliation. Besides, she paid her bills.

Until early January, the Stronach backroom was a modest handful of low-key Conservatives, including Mike Liebrock, a baby-faced former vice president of the Ontario wing who had met Stronach in planning the awards for her "As Prime Minister I Would..." essay-writing contest. He would eventually become her top aide as a Conservative MP Cabinet minister. But the small group was soon overwhelmed by a strike force of seasoned talent quarterbacked by Mike Harris, who placed himself in charge of fundraising.

"It was quite the challenge," Harris recalls. "Everybody asked the same question: 'Does a Stronach really need my money?'"

He reunited his premier's organizational chart to kick-start the cause. Former aides Deb Hutton, Jaime Watt and Anthony Jonker, former chief of staff Guy Giorno, former Mulroney staffer Stewart Braddick and former Cabinet Minister Janet Ecker signed on. Former Preston Manning aides Rick Anderson and Ian Todd fortified the Ontario group. Ralph Klein's former chief of staff Rod Love came aboard to run the Alberta leg of the campaign, and New Brunswick Cabinet Minister Percy Mockler gave the Atlantic campaign a big name.

"We probably didn't give her the advice we should've," confided a top strategist. "Nobody believed she had a chance. She was good for the race, an interesting addition and someone who would add sparkle to something dreary.

There was a paycheque to be made and a lot of fun to be had along the way, but I don't know if anybody was giving her the straight goods."

IF STRONACH WAS A long shot, nobody told the press either. Newspapers were going supernova with front-page speculation on the mysterious blonde billionairess who seemed poised to jazz up what had been a snoozer showdown between sure-bet Stephen Harper and no-chance Tony Clement. In the first 20 days of 2004, Stronach's still-unannounced candidacy rated 37 mentions in the *Toronto Star*, 33 in the *Calgary Herald*, 26 in the *National Post*, 22 in the *Ottawa Citizen* and 19 in the *Montreal Gazette*.

Behind the scenes, her strategists were rushing to piece together a coast-to-coast organization before the Clement camp scooped the best Ontario brains. Stronach brought no political players to the table beyond a mishmash of names she'd collected from social events and philanthropy ventures. She had simply bought a team and handed them the challenge of defining and selling an unknown to the masses in less than two weeks.

The key players had their first brainstorming session less than 10 days before the launch date. Stronach's negatives filled a worrisome half page of internal correspondence: she was "rich, a divorcee, spoiled, a socialite, linked to Clinton, running on a whim, buying the leadership...." The list went on and on. The positives hardly seemed much of an offset: "young, energetic, a woman, a risk-taker, a 'star,' 'sexy,' a moderate with 'real world experience.'"

Alberta's Rod Love was worried enough at the preliminary state of planning to put his concerns in writing.

"With some polishing and a smooth launch, this would get us through the first seven to 10 days. We would be ragging the puck, but getting away with it," he wrote in a memo to Rick Anderson. "But I am still concerned that we need to quickly get her into a policy dip, i.e. 'Ms. Stronach, what is your position on military spending, same-sex marriage, municipal infrastructure, marijuana legislation, mad cow, Burnt Church aboriginal fishing rights, war in Iraq, ad infinitum?' That's what the assholes [that would be reporters] will ask, trying to trip her up early so as to easily dispose of her."

It turned out to be a prophetic fret.

The team took his advice seriously and sat Stronach down for a series of intensive policy briefings and media training. They were astonished by what they found. Instead of the serenely confident corporate president with shareholder-swaying charisma, they were confronted by a nervous, hesitant, unsteady rookie who seemed lacking in any self-assured grasp of basic issues.

"She was much weaker than we thought," confided one strategist. "She could only really stick to a very tight script and repeat it and repeat it. A big weakness was that she hadn't done any thinking about what mattered to her. She'd start to give an answer and Frank [Stronach] would come in and give the rest of the answer. He'd spend more time explaining what her position was than she would because it was his position."

A key part of the battle plan was to get credible names on board to be rolled out as required and when requested. Four Conservative MPs endorsed her bid: Newfoundland's Loyola

Hearn, Manitoba's Inky Mark, Ontario's Gary Schellenberger and Nova Scotia's Bill Casey. But friend and mentor Brian Mulroney was the first in the headlines to polish Stronach's credentials as an outsider with inside-politics potential.

"Our career paths are pretty similar," said Mulroney, the CEO of Iron Ore Company of Canada before making his second attempt at the Progressive Conservative leadership in 1983. "One should not presume that just because a person has not been in the House of Commons, one should not head a parliamentary party, and, in fact, could not do it."

While Mulroney later distanced himself from Stronach's sputtering finish, insisting he never formally endorsed her candidacy, he was effusive in praise for Stronach on the eve of the kickoff.

"If she enters the race, then the Conservative Party is going to be very lucky to get her. She has been a tremendous chief executive officer. She knows how to lead a team. She's disciplined; she's focused; she's a very kind person. She is very bright, very knowledgeable, and she is extremely elegant. An attractive woman of great accomplishment—that's not something that will offend a great many people."

Peter MacKay seemed to jump to her side as well. Harper is "beatable," he said, praising Stronach as someone who is "going to bring a lot of interest, a lot of new people into politics."

Senator Marjory LeBreton, a long-time confidante of Mulroney, told reporters she thought Stronach was only in the race to be a kingmaker at the convention. The next day the phone rang with Stronach asking for her support. The lure of helping a woman was strong, and LeBreton knew it was probably good for the party to have a moderate in the race. She was impressed enough that Stronach had called her directly that she lent her name to the list of supporters, a decision she would later regret.

THERE WERE PLENTY of naysayers to be sure. A Clement adviser christened her "Paul Martin in a cocktail dress" and wondered aloud, "Why would we, as the Conservative Party, pick a leader like her, who cannot attack Martin for being Richie Rich with a private jet and wealthy friends?"

But it was in the media where skepticism raged amid many a caustic reality check against Stronach's imminent race entry.

"She will, of course, be torn to shreds," *Toronto Star* columnist David Olive predicted in a column titled "Just Don't Run, Ms. Stronach," which ran on January 16, 2004, the eve of her entry into Canadian federal politics. It was the best summation of every political shortcoming Stronach would shoulder in the months to follow. "Scan the Stronach resumé and count the ways she's vulnerable. She was born with a silver spoon in her mouth. She's a college dropout. She's not fluent in French. Stronach's flirtation with Olympics reform and a couture house in Toronto are the hallmarks of a dilettante. She has never fought to replace a level rail crossing with an overpass, has never launched a think tank, a food bank or an arts group. Leading as scripted a life as Prince William, Stronach's paucity of major speeches and interviews has made her scarcely a spokeswoman for Magna, much less Canada. Stronach is a figurehead CEO at a company where she was previously occupied, for the most part, with 'non-core' assignments in personnel and philanthropy. Having 'joined Magna at birth,' as she once said, and taken orders from company founder Frank Stronach her entire career, it's fair to ask if Belinda Stronach will be her father's puppet in Ottawa, as well."

Well, ouch. But it was, as it turned out, a fair comment.

Tension was evident inside the team even before the official launch. While Stronach and her Magna cheerleaders were fixated on getting her speech nailed, veterans of various other leadership races insisted she had to prep harder for the follow-up news conference.

"The Q&A with media was where she was vulnerable, but nobody seemed terribly worried about it," one team member confided. The speech was just a reading exercise.

Before making it official, Belinda Stronach had two loose ends to tie up. On January 8, 2004 in the Ontario Superior Court of Justice, Stronach ended her three-year marriage to Norwegian Olympic speed-skating superstar Johann Koss on the grounds of having lived apart for 10 months. Then she quit the CEO position of Magna International and resigned from its board, surrendering the keys to the corporate jet fleet for a life of security checks and middle seats aboard commercial air travel.

AND SO, THE STAGE was set for a quest literally ripped from the pages of her first corporate project at Magna International. That's where a 29-year-old single mother was assigned the job of running her father's new million-dollar Magna for Canada Scholarship Fund. The cornerstone of the project was an essay-writing contest with a $20,000 prize and $50,000 internship. The essay topic: "As Prime Minister I Would...." It would cost her $2.5 million of her own money and a road-wearying 60-day grind under merciless scrutiny, but Belinda Stronach had decided to enter the contest herself as a real-life applicant. Now, Stronach had to articulate what she would do as prime minister if she won.

SEVEN

STRAIGHT FROM
THE HEART

THE STRONACH CAMPAIGN chose the Aurora Legion Hall as its leadership launch pad. They wanted the optics of putting a blue collar on her Valentino fashion image. I talked to Deb, the hall's bar manager, the day before the big event. She could not recall any Stronach having ever setting a Gucci-shoed foot inside the place. And on the day of the declaration, regulars guzzling three-dollar draught told me they'd never before seen a stretch limousine parked in the rear lot.

Every national media outlet had a journalist on the scene to witness the bedlam of Canada's most glamorous political debutante at her coming-out ball. A dozen cameras lined a riser at the back of a room bathed in television lights. The walls were filled with posters that screamed BELINDA in white block letters followed by a lower case .ca to promote her membership-peddling Web site. Some observers felt the pastel backdrop of muted brown, orange, blue and green, selected and produced by Magna's marketing wizards, had been lifted directly from *Martha Stewart Living*. There was no sign of party colours or logos. Her slogan reflected the staccato way Stronach reads a script: "Start. Right. Now."

The crush of reporters kept scanning the crowd for signs of the powerful backers from the Conservative establishment who would turn Harper's leadership cakewalk into a serious contest. Where were they? No sign of former premiers Mike Harris, who had been scheduled to attend, Bill Davis or former Manitoba Premier Gary Filmon. No MPs or senators or party officials turned up to serve in lieu of potted plants as a backdrop. At the last minute, a casually dressed Frank Stronach shuffled in and took a seat beside me as his bodyguards moved into position at the exits. No one had the nerve to tell Magna's founder to leave the seating section reserved for media. Both national news channels went live as Stronach entered from a side door and waded through a throng of perhaps 200 cheering supporters. It took five minutes to reach the microphone where she stood smiling radiantly, dressed in a fitted grey suit and light blue shirt with every strand of blonde hair in place. A few of us noticed her knuckles turning white as she clenched the side of the podium. It took a half a minute or so after the crowd went silent for reporters to figure out why Stronach wasn't speaking as she looked anxiously between glass reflector panels on either side of the stage. The teleprompter, still a rarity used only by federal political leaders after Jean Chrétien's awkward flirtation with the device early in his leadership, was frozen at "Hello," and the highest-profile undeclared candidate for the leadership of the Conservative Party couldn't think of a spontaneous word to say for what seemed like an eternity. It was a bad omen of things to come.

When the technology finally scrolled to life, Stronach recited a business-friendly platform backed by moderate social views. She proposed making mortgage interest partially tax deductible, eliminating the capital tax, joining the United States in a North American security perimeter, increasing military budgets and scrapping the federal gun registry while boosting the sentence for gun crimes. To fund social programs better, "we've got to bake a bigger economic pie," she declared, a quip that would haunt her for years. Marijuana was too dangerous to be decriminalized under a Stronach government, she said, although she admitted to having smoked up in high school. Same-sex marriage was a basic human right she wholeheartedly supported, and her friendship with Bill Clinton was brushed aside as a private matter. Next question, please.

It was all delivered with little passion or flair. Words tumbled out, conviction didn't register. For the media, who have experience in spotting royal jelly in budding politicians, Stronach's grand entrance was a letdown, if not a complete write-off. A perfect political storm of serious money, hefty business credentials and good looks had arrived, but her speech failed to project the most important ingredient of all—human likeability.

CTV news icon Craig Oliver is vision-impaired, but clearly sensed what was unfolding on the legion hall stage and wasn't the slightest bit impressed. He told his viewers it was the worst launch of a leadership he'd ever seen in all his years of covering the federal landscape. Belinda Stronach, he declared, was a dilettante. Out of her league. A disaster in the making. A few days later he cringed when he met Stronach on an Ottawa street corner. Embarrassed at what he readily admits now was an over-the-top blast of negative analysis, he quickly apologized for going too far.

"No worries," Stronach grinned. "How 'bout we get to know each other better over dinner next week?"

REPORTERS HAD BEEN told Frank Stronach would say nothing at the launch lest it steal attention away from his daughter's spotlight. But after she finished her speech and left to prepare for her first media encounter, I turned to him in the seat beside me and threw a softball to see if he'd swing: Well, how'd she do?

"I thought she did good," he said. After that, well, the Magna founder couldn't help himself as reporters swarmed around to hear from the daddy of little girl Belinda.

"She's nobody's little girl, I can assure you of that," he insisted. "The difference between her and me is that I shoot fast from the hip and she would think a bit more and try to find a consensus." Pressed about his daughter's glamorous looks, he shrugged. "If I had a choice, I'd rather be happy, rich and good-looking than poor and sick. The looks should not really matter. It's what you stand for, what you say and what you practise."

Her pro-business platform sounded like a page ripped from Magna's wish list, somebody observed.

"If the economy doesn't function, nothing functions," he continued. "There will be no money for the arts, for social services and so the key question is always how we can make a bigger economic pie."

Well, at least that put to rest any doubt about the origin of Belinda Stronach's signature line in her maiden speech. It was her father who had ghostwritten the phrase that would follow her for the rest of the campaign.

Candidate Stronach survived the news conference without incident and immediately boarded the Belindamobile, a full-sized luxury bus with her photo plastered on both sides, to set out on a national tour with a media entourage in tow. Her first stop: a Winnipeg talk show.

Stronach cringes at the memory, even during an interview two years later.

"I was not at all happy with my performance on the Charles Adler show," she understates.

With good reason. The show opened with Stronach delivering the stammering impersonation of a spaced-out Valley Girl.

"Uh...you know...uh...I...I am very much ready...It's exciting...It's an exciting experience...."

She'd been prepped for weeks, yet Rod Love's prelaunch concerns about her shallow grasp of policy were well founded as she struggled with a simple question on mad cow disease. Pressed on the Liberals' no-go decision on joining the war in Iraq, the would-be prime minister had this comeback: "I don't want to necessarily comment on what I would have done." Asked by a caller to list a shining example of a tough task accomplished while serving as the top executive at Magna International, she stammered a non-answer.

"It was indeed a sad performance. She had the air of someone who has been so over-handled that she has no idea who she herself is or what she thinks," concluded *Globe and Mail* columnist Roy MacGregor. "The result was that she came across as, sorry to have to say this, not very bright."

The often-acerbic Adler later admitted he'd gone easy on Stronach, perhaps out of sympathy for being her first hot-seat interview.

"When media asked me why I soft-balled her," said Adler, "I told them that I didn't want to be accused of shooting Bambi."

The tour lurched on and didn't get much better. Love's team pulled out 1,300 Calgarians to a breakfast event, a record-breaking turnout that forced organizers to find new venues to cope with the huge demand for tickets. Stronach responded with a flat speech that attracted reasonable reviews from the Who's Who crowd of blue-eyed sheiks. But she found herself unable to articulate a position on the Kyoto Accord on climate change, a matter of considerable interest in the oil patch. Then it was off to Vancouver for another cringe-worthy effort where she was tongue-tied during a television newscast by a question on the cause and solution for western alienation. When the tour hit Nova Scotia a few days later, Stronach refused to say where she stood on federal economic development funding for the region.

Watching with alarm from the sidelines via remote control and his network of contacts, Brian Mulroney couldn't take it any longer. He called on friend Mark Entwistle, urging him to dive into a campaign crying out for adult supervision. Entwistle, an easygoing but somewhat low-key personality, is a former diplomat who served briefly as Mulroney's director of communications before being appointed ambassador to Cuba. Legend has it he has sipped many rums with Fidel Castro himself and was credited with keeping a sensitive trade relationship working well under the disapproving eye of the United States. Entwistle reluctantly accepted the assignment of helping someone he'd never met before and finally caught up with Stronach in the business-class cabin of an Air Canada flight somewhere over western Canada. He introduced himself, kicked the travel aide out of a seat across the aisle and sat down. What she needed, he told her bluntly, was a crash course on the issues. Failing that, this campaign was DOA.

Back at her headquarters on St. Clair Avenue in Toronto, their worst fears were being realized. Veterans who had staged her first briefing had desperately hoped Stronach would adjust quickly to the madness of her new environment. They could only shake their heads now. A nervous, unprepared, poorly briefed neophyte was on the loose, armed with only her father's ideas and a few memorized lines for protection with a vigilant, if not vigilante, media horde in pursuit. Her train had left the station all right. The only suspense was the size and scale of the wreck it would become.

VETERAN TOUR ESCORT Deb Hutton laid down two non-negotiable rules for Stronach on the campaign trail: she was never to be left alone with a reporter and she was never to get "shit-faced" with anybody in public. Stronach, by all accounts, complied, often too tired to engage the social circuit in any event. She was, Hutton recalls, a low-maintenance responsibility, never getting testy if the hotel was a Holiday Inn instead of a Hyatt or complaining about food or the long hours. Give Stronach a 5 AM time slot for a workout, and she was happy. But when pushed to explain the stumbles and stutters that seemed to deflate her candidate's first week, Hutton sighed into her Starbucks coffee.

"She functions from an abundance of caution when she's not comfortable. She'd rather say 'I don't know' than to say where she stands. But she didn't get into serious trouble, which is rare for a rookie."

"I told her early on when she was thinking about politics that it was very noble of her, but she was going to be reading a lot of things in the newspapers that would be unpleasant," her father Frank told me. "I said, 'I'm proud of you, but you've got to be very tough.'"

The team quickly learned that Stronach did have serious trouble with speaking French, a phobia that prevented her from including even basic courtesies in her speeches. The campaign deployed so-called demon dialers to blanket specific areas with a recording from the candidate inviting anyone who answers the phone to attend a campaign function or buy a membership. But Stronach was petrified at the prospect of recording even the most basic message in French for her Quebec supporters. What took minutes for a bilingual candidate took hours as Stronach attempted to translate her high school skills into a flawless francophone-friendly message. But her demand for perfection was understandable because a curious outbreak of "Belindamania" was spreading across Quebec. It was a head-scratcher, but the polls showed that the only unilingual anglophone in the race was by far the most popular candidate in the only province with a French-first fixation. A mid-campaign Ipsos-Reid poll gave Stronach 44 percent of Conservative support in Quebec, almost double Harper's number and triple Clement's showing.

"On one of the first trips, we flew into Montreal and went into a room where there were 60–70 people, and she didn't use any French in the speech," recalls Laschinger. "Nobody else could've gotten away with that."

A unilingual candidate in a bilingual country wasn't the only odd angle to her national campaign. Money and media made the Stronach leadership bid dramatically different from any other in recent memory. Money bought her a full national entourage on the grand scale reserved for party leaders during general elections. She had paid staff in regional offices in most major cities and covered the salaries of staff from Navigator Consulting in Toronto. On the tour, there was an advance team, media handlers, a technology assistant, drivers, membership sales co-coordinators, a personal aide and a speechwriter, all under the direction of air traffic control in Toronto where polling was done constantly and translation services were on standby to bridge any language gaps.

Whereas most campaigns round up funding before the spending starts, money was no object from the get-go aboard the Stronach tour, including the regular use of charter aircraft. In Alberta alone, with less than 10 percent of the potential vote at play, money was gushing out of the Stronach campaign coffers at a frantic clip for strategic advice, event planning and hospitality. A Calgary telemarketing firm's estimate to flog $10 memberships to Albertans by phone came in at almost $200,000. The campaign even paid one former party official $1,500 per week with the job description of "driving Harper nuts."

THE MEDIA FASCINATION with Stronach also placed her in decidedly distinct contrast to her headline-deprived rivals.

"When Belinda came in, we were kind of asphyxiated with respect to media attention, and that hurt the fundraising, that hurt the organization," Clement gulped by way of explanation after he finished dead last in the race.

Deb Hutton still shakes her head at the oddity of it all.

"We had way too much media at first," she recalls. "We had to ration her and that's strange, if not unprecedented, for a second- or third-place candidate."

As part of Laschinger's plan to severely limit access to Stronach, christened as the "babe-in-the-bubble" strategy, scrums were limited to one per day, hard-news radio talk shows were overlooked in favour of guest appearances on less intense youth-orientated rock music stations, and one-on-one print media interviews were brief and infrequently granted. In my case, weeks of requests finally produced a 15-minute sit-down chat, which resulted in a January 28 column for the *National Post* and *Calgary Herald*, "Stronach Expresses No Regrets about Running." Major issues were shrugged off, which left little insight beyond this sample exchange:

MARTIN: Is it hard to be a single mom on the road?
STRONACH: No question it's hard to be away from my
    children. I don't view it as being a single parent. I have

a very good relationship with their father, who lives five minutes away. We share the responsibility of raising our children. He's remarried and has two children of his own. My parents live nearby. My kids have a really big family and lots of people around them that love them.

MARTIN: They go to public school, right?

STRONACH: I went to public school, but they go to a private school.

MARTIN: Why's that?

STRONACH: I took a look at the public system and the private school and there were a number of factors. To be honest with you, I did feel they were going to receive a better education and have smaller class sizes. I know it's a provincial matter, but education is so important and the foundation for so many things we need to work together to address these things.

MARTIN: Is your being beautiful an asset or a liability?

STRONACH: Let me ask you. Is being handsome an asset or a liability for a journalist?

MARTIN: I'll ask a handsome journalist.

STRONACH: You're way too hard on yourself, Don. Look, I always think it's good to excite people or inspire people to get involved. If I can help open the door and help encourage people to stay in the party once they walk through that door, I think that's a plus for the party.

MARTIN: Who's your favourite prime minister?

STRONACH: I can't pick one.

MARTIN: Probably be a Conservative, right?

STRONACH: I respect Liberals and Conservatives. I respect

people who stand for something and are willing to get involved and make a difference.

MARTIN: People estimate Paul Martin's worth $50 million. Is he richer or poorer than Belinda Stronach?

STRONACH: We should celebrate individuals who have achieved success in this country and who have made a contribution to Canada. We should have more role models. I don't think we should attack wealth and success in this country. We should celebrate it and attack poverty.

MARTIN: Is the media fixation on your fashion sense starting to fade?

STRONACH: I hope so. I'm running out of shoes for them to write about.

MARTIN: A final question on behalf of all the hot-blooded males around here. Are you dating anyone?

STRONACH: [Laughs] No.

Okay, so it wasn't a probing interview about the weighty issues of the moment—she wasn't answering those questions anyway—but give me some credit for generating a glimpse of warmth behind the frozen mask that Stronach wore throughout the campaign. There seemed to be hope she was getting better.

AND YET, IT WAS falling apart internally. Her campaign headquarters was isolated and ignored by the road show. Her political advisers began to dread their candidate's homecoming trips to "The Compound," as her Aurora residence was dubbed, because it was a sure bet all their input would be systematically scrapped by Frank Stronach or his executive assistant Keith Stein. Magna speechwriters systematically mangled headquarters' efforts. Morale was plunging to new lows daily.

"It was frustrating because we'd be working hard on something and she'd say 'I'm not sure what I think,' and she'd pick up the phone and call somebody and half an hour later 10 friends of hers would show up and come into the political discussion to give their own advice," said one senior official with the campaign.

With the cut-off for membership sales looming and the tour stagnating, Stronach's handlers made a curious call: They refused to allow Stronach to participate in three television-network debates. That left a pair of party-sanctioned debates carried on the low-rated parliamentary channel as the only opportunities for the public to see their candidate in action. To prepare for the first showdown on February 22, Stronach hired communications consultant Barry McLoughlin to whip her into shape. McLoughlin's a polished veteran of the media relations and public presentation game in Ottawa and his rates are among the highest in the business, notwithstanding that he'd coached former Alliance Leader Stockwell Day for his disastrous performance in the 2000 election debate. But even with his help, her team decided she needed more intensive prepping before facing off against her two more experienced opponents, so they set up a role-playing exercise with hired guns as stand-ins for Harper and Clement. The fake leaders did such an outstanding job of slicing and dicing a bamboozled Stronach in the mock debate that she finally lost her cool and terminated the exercise.

"She kept getting choked up on her answers and finally wouldn't do it," confides a witness to the exercise. "We told her, 'You have to be caught flat-footed to see what it's like so when it happens you know the way out.' But she'd had enough."

Thus, Stronach had cause to be nervous on debate night at the Ottawa Congress Centre for the trio's first war of words. To make matters more daunting, it was the last debate before membership sales would be cut off a week later. She had to set herself above and apart from her rivals to get member support on a dramatic growth spurt or all was lost.

"I am not a professional politician," she declared by way of differentiation. "That makes me the only candidate who can still see things from a citizen's perspective."

That line brought giggles from the assembled media, who felt her former million-dollar-per-month paycheque hardly qualified her as having an average citizen's perspective. The debate raged on, featuring petulant shots by Clement at Stronach's potential conflicts as a Magna heiress, which, in hindsight, were a tad rich given her Magna wealth helped bail Clement out of campaign debt a few months later. But Clement knew the guy to beat wasn't a blonde, so he saved his harshest attacks for Harper, accusing his future prime minister of building walls and division within the country and of failing to gain support in the key Ontario stronghold during his two years as leader.

"What does your record show?" Clement shouted.

"The record shows I'm the only one on the stage that's won an election in the last two years," Harper responded icily. "Get yourself elected to the national Parliament, then give me the lecture, okay?"

While no candidate shone with intellectual brilliance or ignited oratorical fire, the reviews on Stronach's performance were particularly harsh.

"There's just no spontaneity there at all," lamented Ipsos-Reid pollster Darrell Bricker during a debate analysis. "It's like she's putting a tape into her head every time she answers a question."

Toronto Star columnist Chantal Hébert weighed in with a devastatingly blunt assessment of Stronach's stiff and scripted look on February 23 in "Liberal Fall Hurts Stronach Too": "Stronach did not help herself with a performance that was short on specifics and long on rehearsed responses. After a month on the campaign trail, she still cannot say whether she would have committed troops to the Iraq war. She still lists her lack of political experience as her top asset. When it was over, she was asked by reporters if she had been getting instructions from her handlers through her earpiece. For the record, the answer is no. But the fact the question was asked speaks volumes as to the karaoke flavour of parts of her performance."

Susan Riley of the *Ottawa Citizen* is rarely caustic in her analysis and tends to seek positives in women politicians, but she was inconsolable after watching Stronach on the set: "The profoundly unready Stronach, who churned out pre-digested paragraphs on various topics with the monotonous predictability of a sausage machine, is praised for surviving," she wrote in her February 23 column, "Belinda Bombs, Party Loses." "She did not swear, or freeze, or stumble (much)—or, for that matter, show anything resembling spontaneous emotion—and, for this, she is allowed to continue to promulgate the illusion that she deserves to be prime minister. 'Give me 40 days in the campaign trenches with Paul Martin and I'll give you the keys to 24 Sussex,' she declared. In the real world, the only reasonable response to this nonsense would be an incredulous laugh."

KNOCKED BACK ON its heels with only days to go before membership sales closed, the Stronach team decided it needed a "kick ass" speech to invigorate the campaign. They picked a powerhouse setting, the Canadian Club and Empire Club of Toronto, and decided to aim for the largest crowd the paired clubs had ever attracted. The best speechwriters in the Canadian Conservative world went to work crafting a "seminal" piece of visionary work.

"It was a pivotal point. We were not going to just pull a speech out of our asses," recalls one who worked on the address. "It was the most prestigious platform we could find at a pivotal point in the campaign." He pauses. "Then the rewrite crew headed by Keith Stein got into the act and rewrote in every cliché they could find."

Stronach has a different take of the "seminal" result and defends her pal Stein from criticism.

"I kept telling the campaign, 'What is this shit?' I'm not going to say something from a wedge position to drive something between myself and the other candidates. It was a frustrating final two or three weeks. The speeches weren't me, they were not as thoughtful."

Not that what she eventually delivered was a beacon of visionary illumination. Her mortified campaign advisers winced at the back of the room when she launched into the revised text.

"I've been called the 'It Girl' of the political right, Magna Spice and Bionic Stronach...a dishy blonde and Paul Martin in a cocktail dress," Stronach told a crowd of 1,000, which fell short of their record-setting target but easily beat the combined attendance for Harper and Clement speeches a week earlier. "Bottom line, I understand the economy," Stronach continued. "I understand what it takes to create jobs, to spend money wisely and to invest in the future."

The standing ovation and generally supportive reviews from the crowd allowed Stronach to claim some momentum back in their camp, but it was short-lived.

A first-ballot defeat to Harper became increasingly obvious toward the end of February, so the campaign shifted into desperation mode. A Belinda National House Party was planned, where hundreds of hosts would invite a dozen or so potential members into their homes for coffee and, at the pre-arranged time, dial into a conference centre to hear a pep talk from Stronach. Around the same time, Magna went partisan, unleashing the inevitable arm-twisting of its Canadian workforce through a letter from executive vice-chairman Manfred Gingl. Managers were told to remind their employees about the leadership race and to urge them to buy memberships because "Belinda needs our help," he wrote. Even the weather turned against the tour. An ice storm hit southwestern Ontario leaving Stronach stranded on the highway with 300 supporters waiting for her at a London, Ontario event. Not wanting to write off the night as a total loss, organizers beamed Stronach's disembodied voice over a speakerphone to the gathering. More than a few in the crowd compared the experience to a bad episode of *Charlie's Angels*.

Party membership list irregularities also surfaced which seemed to go against the Stronach camp. A furious Laschinger demanded the entire leadership vote be delayed to deal with the scandal. It was, of course, a massive overreaction, and it soon appeared the Stronach campaign was throwing stones in its own glass house of membership shenanigans. Members of the Gespeg First Nations in Quebec complained their names appeared on the list of new Conservative members recruited by Stronach without ever having signed up.

Speculation started to swirl that wholesale changes were about to be made at the top as Belinda Stronach retreated more and more into the realm of faithful friends and family for guidance. Her daily blog fell silent and the Belindamobile, which had been packed with media tagalongs at the start, was down to a lonely wire service reporter and one Global National camera crew as the finish line approached.

But the truly bad news was just developing in, of all places, the friendly shadows of Magna's world headquarters—a suspicion (if not a reality) that would incubate into one of the great political hatreds of all time on Parliament Hill. Stephen Harper, it seemed, was waging personal warfare against Belinda Stronach.

It started with an urgent phone call from Sheila Pearce, who was supervising the local Newmarket–Aurora riding contest for the Conservative nomination. It was considered a no-brainer, a safe bet that Stronach's money and organizational muscle would squash musician Lois Brown's challenge for the right to carry Conservative colours into the next election. But Pearce had an ominous feeling as she tapped into rising support for Brown on the doorstep and pushed the panic button.

"Sheila called and told me to get back to the local riding to sign up members right away," Stronach remembers. "She was worried I'd left it too late. Laschinger had said there was no problem and that everything was okay. Well, it wasn't. It was much closer than anybody anticipated."

Blame for the shift seemed obvious to everyone in the Stronach camp. The guy behind the grassy knoll, trying to take out his main rival, had to be Stephen Harper.

Harper operatives were seen working at Brown headquarters. Endorsements from the former leader appeared on Brown's campaign literature. Her staff wore Harper T-shirts.

"Belinda was appalled," recalls Entwistle. "She was running for the leadership, and the leader of the party is supposed to be neutral. Yet here was Harper, saying 'I want her and not the blonde one.' It was galling, and that's when Belinda realized this relationship was going to be more difficult. There was an edge, a harshness, and there's no doubt the Harper people came in and worked the riding with their resources."

B.C. MP John Cummins was convinced enough to fire off a scathing Dear Stephen missive, expressing disappointment in the conspiracy to dump Stronach in her local riding.

"What does the decision to intervene say about your leadership style? What does it say about your commitment to uniting the new party? By stepping into the race to endorse her opponent, you are saying that as party leader you would not want Ms. Stronach on your team as a candidate or in your caucus as an MP."

His protests were pooh-poohed by Harper sidekick John Reynolds.

"I am unaware of any formal endorsement that Stephen has made of Lois Brown's candidacy in Newmarket–Aurora," Reynolds snapped back. "All that had been issued was a generic 'statement' from Harper saying that Brown, who had won an Alliance nomination prior to the merger, would make 'a fine parliamentarian,'" Reynolds said. "I would urge you not to twist the facts for the purposes of division during this critical time. All our guns need to be directed at the Liberals, not at each other, at this very exciting time."

Stronach's top advisers had an ominous feeling as they tried to find a place to park outside Aurora High School on the evening of March 9, 2004. Cars sprawled for what seemed like miles in every direction. It was the sign of a hotly contested fight. Sure enough, the gymnasium was packed with more than 1,000 locals almost equally divided between the two camps, both sides trying to drown each other out.

"It was a freak show. I thought we'd lost that night," recalls strategist Jaime Watt.

The consequences of such a shocking upset were almost too catastrophic for campaign brass to contemplate. After two months of national exposure and intensive media hype, Watt and Laschinger stood at the back of the room wondering what to do if their candidate finished second. Earlier in the day, Laschinger had told Frank Stronach to stay home lest he become a distraction.

"I don't need your vote," he told the father of the candidate.

Now Laschinger wasn't so sure. Both men knew their campaign for a national title would be fatally wounded if Stronach couldn't claim the Conservative ballot box slot in Aurora. If the speeches that night were any indication, Brown appeared set to win. The former Alliance Party diehard proudly proclaimed no interest in being the leader, merely pledging to do her best as the area's local MP. It was a crowd-pleasing position, and Stronach seemed to misread the mood by delivering a stock speech on why she wanted to be Conservative leader. In the end, after a long, agonizing wait for the votes to be counted, Stronach beat Brown by 100 votes—512 to 412. It was a near-death experience and Stronach knew it. Publicly, she called it the first of three steps to achieving her goal. Her next task was to win the leadership before forming a Conservative government. Privately, as she eyed another batch of itineraries for the final push ahead, Stronach resolved to never again take the local vote for granted while touring the country.

WITH A WEEK TO go before the March 20 vote, Stronach cornered Laschinger, a serious look on her weary face.

"Is there a chance?" she asked point-blank. Laschinger had read new polls showing Harper with a commanding 20-point lead among Conservatives. He shook his head.

"We have to be realistic," he replied. "No, there isn't."

Undeterred, Stronach hit the road for what was billed as a final barnstorming blitz, but few media bothered to join what was so clearly a doomed effort as it rolled over southwestern Ontario before shrinking crowds. Reporters on the bus reported a smell of defeat, if not death, as the Belindamobile limped toward Toronto for her last gasp shot at winning over the membership. It was too late, but at least they hoped she'd go out with more bang than whimper.

Stronach had drawn the short straw to speak first in the cavernous convention hall on a blustery March 20, 2004. Still ill at ease at talking before large public gatherings, she cancelled a pre-speech rally with supporters and brushed off a planned media appearance to focus on rehearsing her speech, leaving Laschinger to hold court for reporters covering the convention.

He pulled up a chair, turned it around and straddled it with his oversized frame. All that was missing was an oversized cigar and a tumbler of Scotch to complete the picture of the consummate backroom player at work. Media moved in with tape recordings running. They asked about the highlight of the campaign.

"It's been a blur," he snapped. "Something like Alphonso Gagliano's memory."

Reporters exchanged knowing glances. Lasch was testy. And a testy Lasch gives a good quote. So what about Stronach's performance as a rookie candidate?

"She hasn't made a single bone, boner. I shouldn't have used that word," he winced.

Could she run the country? another asked.

"I've been watching Paul Martin for three months, and I think anybody could run the country better than him."

That, a third scribe noted, wasn't exactly a "ringing endorsement" of his candidate.

"Next," Laschinger snarled.

SHE WOULD PRETEND TO say it straight from her heart. It was her dad's idea, actually. For the grand finale of her campaign to become leader of the Conservative Party, Belinda Stronach would take a portable microphone, walk to centre stage and start speaking without a teleprompter's stilting, stifling impact. No notes. No text for the reporters to follow along. It would showcase her confident sincerity, unscripted passion for the job and give her a human touch, Frank Stronach had told John Laschinger two days before his daughter was to address the convention. By then, the disappointingly low number of Stronach membership sales had sealed her fate. A shocking come-from-behind victory was no longer an option. "Two days before the vote, Frank Stronach phones me with this great idea for her to do the convention without notes, impromptu," Laschinger recalls. "I told him, 'Frank, she's going to do well, but she's not going to win it, so if she feels comfortable, let's do it.'" Stronach didn't wing it entirely, of course. Curled up in her palm was a piece of paper with a few memory-jogging lines scribbled on it. Just in case.

"I should've done it without the cue cards," she recalled ruefully two years later.

Her costly entourage of professional tour organizers hadn't been consulted nor had they approved the unusual finale. Their input had been displaced by family and friends weeks earlier. The pros had retreated to the headquarters to write up their invoices for services rendered and often ignored. Frank Stronach, Magna executive Keith Stein and media pal Arlene Bynon were in cruise control as the Belindamobile limped toward the convention in downtown Toronto on March 20, 2004.

Her speech would be delivered on the very same Toronto Convention Centre stage where, just 10 months earlier, Stronach had watched Peter MacKay join forces with anti-free-trader David Orchard to win the Progressive Conservative leadership over Jim Prentice and future fellow turncoat Scott Brison.

Two hours before her speaking time, Stronach descended an escalator into the waiting arms of former Ontario premiers Mike Harris and Bill Davis before disappearing into her hospitality suite en route to the stage. Several aides had tried to talk her into modifying the speaking strategy a bit, to say she was going to talk from her heart, but admit to having point-form cue cards in hand lest she be hit by stage fright. Their advice was ignored. Admitting to human frailties is never an option in Stronach minds.

At 8 PM, she hit the stage in a dazzling white Valentino pantsuit with a pink ribbon and a pair of gold shoes fashion commentators figured cost more than the entire bid of rival Tony Clement.

"Tonight I threw away my formal text and I'm here speaking to you from the heart," Stronach told the crowd. "They tell me that I'm Paul Martin in a cocktail dress. But let me ask you: Who can bake a better economic pie?"

There were groans from rival supporters in the crowd.

"We have one common goal and that is to get rid of the tired old Liberal government," she continued, taking a quick glance at her hand. "Canadians have had enough of politics as usual. In fact, I've had enough of politics as usual. To Paul Martin, you cannot run from your own track record. You cannot run against the Chrétien government. Paul Martin would like us to believe that he was a stowaway on the good ship Chrétien when in fact he was its first mate. As the former CEO of a corporation, if I ran my company the way that Paul Martin ran the finances of this country, we would have had a major shareholder revolt. Either Paul Martin was part of the shameful mess or he is incompetent. Either way, he isn't fit to be the prime minister of Canada."

And then it was over. A gas-fired gun discharged thousands of streams of coloured paper across the stage. It was an expensive bang for a lot of bucks. Convention centre management charges anyone who discharges a confetti or paper gun $5,000 for the privilege of complicating their cleanup job.

"The view persisted she could move the convention if the right speech was delivered. It was adequate, but not enough," remembers Deb Hutton.

Still, Stronach wound up her campaign the way it had been planned from the start. She spared rivals the brunt of her attack and savaged Paul Martin with accusations that became infinitely more interesting after the seismic defection that rattled Ottawa 14 months later. Behind the scenes, invoices were flooding into fax machines at Stronach headquarters. A campaign that had cost more than the combined tab of both rivals was finally over. The only outstanding part of the campaign now was accounts payable.

HARPER CLINCHED A first-ballot victory with 55.5 percent
of the 94,000 members who bothered to vote from a total
membership of 253,000. Stronach finished second with 35
percent of the total while Tony Clement finished a distant
third with 9.5 percent of the ballots. The earlier polls had
been bang on. Harper handily won the West and Ontario,
while Stronach did surprisingly well in Atlantic Canada and
claimed 60 percent of the support in Quebec. Tony Clement
fizzled everywhere. Six months later, Stronach took pity and
cut him a $100,000 cheque to help pay off his $470,000 campaign debt.

When it came time for the obligatory acts of praise for
rivals to unify the convention behind the new leader, Harper
couldn't bring himself to be totally magnanimous.

"Belinda played a significant and crucial role in the
establishment of our new party," he said in his victory speech.
"And, dare I say, she generated significantly more glamour
than I was able to."

It was a backhanded compliment some interpreted to
mean that Belinda brought style while he brought substance.
Or perhaps not. But even opponents credit Stronach with
creating the public and media attention that produced
130,000 new party members.

The final item of business for the Stronach campaign
after the ballots were destroyed was to party. The group
adjourned to a cozy upstairs room at the Indian Motorcycle
Cafe on Toronto's trendy King Street, a safe distance from
the gloomy convention centre. Clement supporters could be
seen guzzling free booze in the crowd, but Harper supporters
boycotted the event, perhaps sensing the showdown to come.

While the defeated candidate gamely mingled with her loy-
alists at one end of the room, Frank Stronach was surrounded
by fawning women at the bar.

"I pay taxes in three countries," he joked. "Everyone
wants my money."

THE DAY AFTER the voting, Stronach's campaign received its
first and only call from the Harper camp. It had nothing to
do with congratulations for their candidate's gutsy performance or attention-grabbing campaign contribution. The top
Harper aide had one simple question: How did Belinda get all
that media coverage as an untried, untested, heck, unelected
politician? Stronach's people shook their heads as they hung
up the phone.

"I LIKE HER AND STILL LIKE HER," Laschinger said in late
2005. "I've never seen anyone make such an improvement in
Canadian politics in such a short time since Pierre Elliott
Trudeau."

While he holds no bitterness about the campaign or
Stronach's subsequent defection to the Liberals, bad feelings
linger in others who worked the campaign and felt their
input was ignored.

"Forcing Harper to win on the second ballot would've
been a victory for us," one key strategist says. "We worked hard
from the beginning so she wouldn't become a laughingstock."

The architects of the Mike Harris and Ralph Klein revo-
lutions had put their names to a grand makeover experiment,

trying to leapfrog a boardroom heiress directly into a national party leader's office in less than 100 days. In the end, with the results falling short of expectations and the candidate bowing out, having brought glamour but few new ideas to the race, the ignored experts felt it was them who had become the laughingstock.

But clearly a greater good was served by having Belinda Stronach in the race beyond merely adding sizzle. By running with such fierce determination at considerable personal sacrifice, Stronach had raised the stakes.

"Belinda challenging Stephen makes it a legitimate win," argues Jaime Watt. "The prize Harper won was better for her having been in it. She gave him a gift."

Nobody knew it at the time, but it wouldn't be the last time Stronach inadvertently helped Harper by seeming to act against him. Her encore performance was just over one year away.

EIGHT

SIMMERING
AMBITION

H E SAT QUIETLY NEXT to her on the second floor of Di Nardo's, an upscale reception hall in Aurora. Frank Stronach knew what his daughter was going through. He tried to console her as she twitched nervously in front of the television, but wasn't sure this night would have a happy ending. These same voters had done it to him 16 years earlier. Belinda Stronach was losing her first election in the very same riding as he did in 1988. Her bid to swap a corporate throne for a political Commons was in extreme jeopardy.

A disappointing national picture was emerging for her party in the June 28, 2004 vote. The Liberals had been downgraded to a minority government, and the 905 area code had not, as expected, swept into the Conservative fold. As the 11 o'clock news hit the screen, the fight for Newmarket–Aurora was still too close to call. A frantic Stronach was trailing her

Liberal rival by a couple hundred votes and running out of unreported polls to reverse the result.

National network crews were on standby downstairs in a ballroom bathed in television lights, waiting to capture the moment the Stronach Curse would become a two-time trend and put to rest the prospect of Magna-made MPs. Outside the hall, trusted aide Sheila Pearce was feeling nauseous as she greeted a stream of poll captains showing up for the "victory" party, all of them reporting loss after loss in their supposedly safe polls.

"This is just like what happened to Frank," noted Joyce Belcourt, the long-time friend who had taught Belinda Stronach to change diapers as a young mother, as she watched it unfold in the headquarters. Co-workers begged her not to raise that spectre again.

It was inexplicable. Belinda Stronach was the hometown girl up against Liberal parachute candidate Martha Hall Findlay. Her father's Magna International was the region's largest employer, which poured thousands of fat paycheques into the Toronto bedroom community's economy. Besides, a local poll had given her a 20-point lead only two weeks earlier. There could be only one person to blame: Stephen Harper.

The Conservative leader's odd behaviour of late, withdrawing into a shell and babbling about bringing the West back into Ottawa while touring his Alberta fortress, had cooled her reception at the doorsteps. Paul Martin's campaign of fear against the Conservatives as the Antichrists of human rights and health care was also working, and a few renegade MPs from her own party were feeding the Neanderthal image with off-script social conservative banter.

There was only one hope left. The advance polls are the last votes to be counted on election night, and those were stuffed into ballot boxes during a week when the Conservatives were doing better. Before their demons were resurrected. Before voter doubts resurfaced.

When Stronach gets apprehensive, she goes very, very quiet. For three hours she bit her fingernails and stared at the television screen while the campaign team relayed grim news from the field. It wasn't until 11:30 PM, when the advance polls started rolling in, that she edged into the lead. Downstairs, where a crowd of 750 people had expected to start a lavish victory party at 9:30 PM featuring the rock group Glass Tiger and unlimited free booze, there was finally something to whoop about.

At five minutes past midnight, Stronach was the final Ontario Conservative to be declared elected with a 700-vote margin of victory. The new MP for Newmarket–Aurora picked up her victory speech, smoothed out her pink suit and signalled aides to have Aurora Mayor Tim Jones begin her introduction. As she walked toward the stairs leading down to the hall, she turned to her friends and said, "I'd rather go through childbirth than go through that again."

Invigorated temporarily by the euphoric crowd, Stronach strayed from her text.

"I don't know about you, but I've got no fingernails left. I would like to say three things to the people of Newmarket and Aurora; thank you, thank you," she hesitated, "and thank you."

Exhausted and drained by her near-death entry into federal politics, a dazed Stronach didn't last long at her own $100,000 victory party before heading home to bed.

EVEN BEFORE THE campaign officially started the day after the May long weekend, Stronach had been invited to wave the Conservative flag in dozens of swing ridings across the country. At least one MP didn't need her help, but she went anyway, flying to Nova Scotia to see Peter MacKay. Some whisper it was there and then their romantic relationship was consummated, although others insist that was impossible because MacKay was happily attached to girlfriend Lisa Merrithew at the time. In any event, Stronach can't remember when things got hot and heavy with MacKay. Sometime during or just after the election, she says.

After the writ dropped, every day brought another parade of curious journalists to Stronach's office seeking interviews or permission to tag along on the campaign trail. National networks regularly carried live hits from the riding, highly unusual attention for a rookie, but feeding an almost insatiable public interest in this particular candidate. Watching carefully from the other side of the fence was Kyle Peterson, campaign manager for Hall Findlay. Stronach was getting a lot better, he noted with some concern. She was looser in approaching people, open to improvisation in speeches and handled the media throng with greater aplomb.

"We were not fighting against that Conservative who was on stage at the leadership convention talking about baking a bigger economic pie," Peterson recalls. "I was kind of hoping that was who we'd get in the election. It would've made things a lot easier."

The only hiccups she encountered on the hustings seemed to be concerns from women who feared Harper had a secret pro-life, anti-gay, private-health agenda. So when

Harper paid a courtesy call on June 9, seemingly to put aside any lingering bad blood from the leadership race, Stronach privately felt he was more of a liability than an asset. Her name recognition was higher than his in the riding, and she had big money to spend on fielding the best tactical assault team ever assembled for a first-time hopeful.

The local campaign was basically a microcosm of the federal election battlefield. She attacked the Liberals for corruption on the sponsorship file and gutting public health care. The Liberals fought back with warnings of a secret Conservative health-privatization agenda, which Hall Findlay gleefully hammered home by pointing out Magna's plans to build its own health clinic, complete with helipad, for employees. Stronach had one clear edge. She was born, raised and still lived in the riding while Hall Findlay had only returned as a renter two months before the election.

Without a Conservative controversy to undermine what would end up becoming a $241,000 campaign, more than double what her Liberal rival would spend, Stronach seemed set to pole-vault into a Commons seat. A national pollster paused to check out the pulse of her riding and quickly moved on to closer and more interesting races. COMPAS Inc. found Stronach was favoured by 59 percent of local voters compared to 30 percent for the Liberals' Hall Findlay. It appeared that a massacre was in the making.

She's a "formidable candidate," decreed poll firm president Conrad Winn. "Her profile as a national leadership contender has allowed her to take an astronomical number and make it even higher."

Well, oops. Stronach had in fact lost the election-day vote. Her squeak to victory was dependent on a 1,000-vote lead in the advance poll.

"It was the most gut-wrenching experience of my political life, and my first campaign was in 1974," recalls campaign manager Rob Sinclair. He sat in the command centre before a colour-coded map trying to make sense of the results as they poured in—and couldn't. "Our strong areas were weak and our weak areas were strong. The most affluent part of Aurora voted Liberal. Belinda went over well in new Canadian areas, but all the university-educated districts went out the back door," Sinclair recalls. "What the hell happened? Well, when traditional voting patterns go out the window, you end up with what happened in Newmarket–Aurora in 2004."

Hall Findlay was magnanimous in defeat, but felt Stronach's 689-vote win was almost a moral victory given her distant come-from-behind status. Still, there was a perversely twisted irony in her near future. The twist was how she'd reclaim the right to tackle Stronach under the Liberal banner the following spring and, on the day before her campaign kickoff barbecue, would be arbitrarily booted out of the party lineup to make way for...Belinda Stronach. And the irony was that it would take her 2004 Conservative rival to ultimately reclaim the seat for the Liberals in 2006. Politics doesn't get any more perverse than that.

THE ELECTION RESULT put Conservative leader Stephen Harper into a dark funk. On the campaign jet returning to

Ottawa from Calgary the day after the vote, reporters' jaws dropped when he opened the door to his possible resignation. At his first caucus meeting after the vote, he again admitted to lingering uncertainty about plans to lead the party into another election. Perhaps, he muttered, a new leader was needed. Several MPs took him aside after that to warn him never to show self-doubt in front of his MPs again, if only to preserve party morale.

Low morale was not an issue for Stronach, who quietly watched Harper's lament from the back of the room. Hearing him muse about a snap resignation was one of those hold-those-horses moments, a hint she might get to take another shot at the leadership much sooner than any-body expected. Only several months later, after Harper confirmed his intention to lead for another election, did Stronach shift her idling machine into park. But she never did turn off the engine.

Stronach went invisible for the rest of 2004, saying nothing in caucus and making only periodic noise in the Commons. You could always tell when she had won a slot in the Question Period lineup. She'd take her seat beside former Canadian Alliance Leader Stockwell Day, put the script neatly on her desk and silently rehearse the ques-tion, her lips moving, head nodding and taking pains to practise looking up at the minister across the aisle she would fearlessly challenge when the Speaker activated her mike.

Being International Trade critic set up one of those hap-penstance encounters that, with the benefit of hindsight, is such a serendipitous part of Stronach's life. The Liberal

Cabinet minister she was assigned to attack was Jim Peterson. His brother, former Ontario Premier David Peterson, would play a pivotal role in luring Stronach across the floor in the year ahead.

THERE WERE SUBTLE signs her leadership ambitions were merely dormant, not dead. Sheila Pearce recalls being so exhausted that she was almost bedridden at the end of the election campaign, which ended six solid months of frantic activity. But after recovering and enjoying an opulent spa retreat paid for by her grateful boss, Stronach had another assignment for her.

"She sent out 10,000 Christmas cards that year to every single person who helped in her campaign and Christmas arrangements across the country," she says. "I spent six weeks compiling the lists."

The floral bouquets were impressive to recipients who felt they hadn't done much to deserve it. Many marvelled at the generosity of the gesture. A few wondered if there was a catch.

At the January 2005 Conservative caucus retreat in Victoria, same-sex marriage hogged the agenda as Paul Martin rattled his sabre with talk of calling a snap election to defend what he described as a Charter right. He didn't much care that the Supreme Court had declined to rule on the issue's constitutionality. It was a political wedge against the Conservatives, so he intended to pound it between the two parties with a pile driver.

Belinda Stronach was in high demand from journalists as

a proud critic of the party's stand against gay or lesbian marriages. Harper saw it coming as he dug in his heels to defend the institution as limited to opposite-sex unions.

"I fully expect that any member of the party who disagrees with that position will become a media star in the next few weeks," he told reporters.

Sure enough, Stronach became a headline when she wrinkled her nose at a series of ethnic media newspaper ads promoting the Conservatives' firm orientation toward a traditional definition of marriage.

"I would not have run the ads," she sniffed. "The leader has the right to indicate what his views are, but...I believe it's an equal rights issue."

Perhaps to increase Harper's paranoia, word was spreading that she was engaged in a secret torrid romance with Peter MacKay. And, sure enough, there was his deputy leader huffing into microphones that he had never been consulted about the ad campaign either. Too bad, Harper told me in an interview at the time, "I've never considered caucus a focus group for advertising."

Stronach joined me for lunch in Victoria's Empress Hotel during the retreat and used selective silences to convey her displeasure with the party position against same-sex marriages. I pushed her on the impact it was going to have on the party's electoral magnetism in Toronto and the youth vote she'd been trying to attract. She pressed her lips and stayed mum. Feeling mischievous, I asked about the legitimacy of Harper embracing this issue with such fervent passion before it had been formally ratified by the membership at a policy convention.

"I'm eating my soup," she said, deliberately saying nothing more.

And, I wondered, how would Stronach possibly get re-elected as a Conservative in the 905 if same-sex marriage became a defining election issue?

"Why do you think I'm speaking out?" she blurted with obvious exasperation. "Sure it's going to be more challenging in urban centres, including the GTA. There's a greater diversity of views here."

As she gathered her belongings to catch a red-eye night flight to Ottawa, Stronach handed me her BlackBerry showing the results of a new poll. It had 71 percent of Canadians in favour of same-sex marriages versus 27 percent against.

"So what does that tell you about the Conservative Party's position?" I asked Stronach.

"Gotta run," she said with a frown.

It was a quiet rebel yell, but the message was loud and clear. Belinda Stronach was starting to feel uncomfortable in her party's skin.

THEY HAD IT A tad backwards. Create the new party. Choose the new leader. Then run an election campaign. Finally, figure out what the new party stood for. Such was the predicament facing the reunited Conservative Party of Canada in the early spring of 2005 as it prepared for its founding policy convention a full 15 months after it was born.

If Stephen Harper suspected Stronach of conspiring for his leadership in Victoria, he would've cried assassin at what was going on behind the grassy knolls that shield the Magna golf course from public view. Inside the clubhouse about a month before the March convention, a private meeting was convened by Belinda Stronach. John Laschinger, political mentor Bill Davis and a pollster were there along with some logistics organizers.

Their mission was simple. Quietly position Stronach as a moderate leader-in-waiting and make darn sure she wasn't caught without an answer to policy questions. Their plans called for a dozen workers equipped with two-way communication to fan out across the convention hall. Every debate, every decision, every corridor flare-up was to be monitored and developments communicated to the operations centre immediately. There, Laschinger would assess the information and relay any data to Stronach he felt she needed for public comment, if requested.

"They wanted to make sure she wasn't blindsided by something happening at the convention she didn't know about," said one of the observers at the meeting. "It was very organized, very efficient, almost military-like. Everybody knew what the other guy was doing. There was a Stronach war room right there at the convention."

This was not, by the way, standard political procedure for MPs. It's doubtful Harper himself had such an elaborate network feeding him data from the convention floor.

"This looked to me like it was all about future planning and the 'next phase,'" the observer said.

AT THE PRE-CONVENTION meeting, Stronach listened and accepted the seasoned advice of her team on all but one point. She wanted to host the mother of all hospitality suites in Old Montreal, not far from her apartment. Laschinger and Davis argued against it.

"It'll make you look like you're running for the leadership," they warned her. "People will get jealous and suspicious of your motives."

Stronach would not be deterred.

"People are going to be watching this," she insisted, "and we have to prove we're not the staid old Reform Party. We've got to have some fun and liven things up."

She arrived at the Montreal Convention Centre on March 17, 2005, wearing a green leather Hugo Boss jacket in a tip 'o the hat to St. Patrick's Day, and was one of the last of 2,000 delegates to register. She wasn't terribly happy despite receiving a warm reception from the crowd. Her offer to address the troops had been rejected.

"She's not being treated as a demi-goddess within the party," one sarcastic official confided to the *Toronto Star*'s Tonda McCharles. "She wants some kind of Celine Dion–type role."

Being offered the chance to introduce a visiting Conservative MPP simply wasn't what Stronach had in mind. She wanted to showcase substance, not serve as window dressing.

"Actions speak louder than words," she complained to McCharles. "From day one I've been nothing but supportive of Stephen, and I've put in a lot of personal effort to see that this party grows and gets stronger, that we mature and dismiss the idea of a hidden agenda."

It had the ring of a diva with big ambition. And to worsen matters, her out-in-the-open lover was making life difficult for Stephen Harper.

MacKay had gone postal against a motion by Ontario MP Scott Reid, one of Harper's closest advisers, which proposed to amend the terms of the merger to curtail the number of future convention delegates from ridings with less than 100 members. It seemed reasonable to many Conservatives. Any shell of a riding with less than 100 party members arguably didn't deserve the same convention weight as an Alberta riding with thousands of true blue faithful. But MacKay, doing his best imitation of David Orchard in full betrayal fury, argued the original deal would be compromised and demanded Harper kill the motion. An emergency caucus meeting was convened, and MacKay stormed out to hint at leading a breakaway PC party if the move wasn't quashed.

It was but a sideshow and was ultimately resolved to MacKay's satisfaction, but a negative media story hijacked the positive vibes of the convention on its first day. Be it MacKay's rant or seeing a well-informed Stronach talking into any microphone within reach, Harper was seething to himself behind the curtains. His anger manifested itself in a chair-kicking tantrum. Unfortunately, he chose to do it within eyesight of reporters, who gleefully spread word that Harper was on a rampage.

THE STRONACH COMMUNICATIONS network worked well. She took the convention microphone to speak on four issues, which solidified her position as a voice of youthful moderation. She supported same-sex marriages, abortion rights, youth representation and the environment. Outside the meeting rooms, she was a convention sensation, getting stopped for photos every dozen steps and being ambushed for a valiant singing stint on Rick Mercer's *Monday Report*.

"Some of the people I was with said, 'Don't go up on same-sex, think about the future,'" Stronach recalls. "I said, 'Shit, I gotta go up there. Otherwise, I couldn't live with myself.'"

The convention itself moved the Conservatives more into the mainstream by abandoning abortion legislation and defending public health care. But there remained strong support for the traditional definition of marriage. Ironically, some of the democratic ideas that initially appealed to Stronach when she first met Reform Leader Preston Manning were jettisoned, including fixed election dates, the use of referendum and MP recall.

She was right about the hospitality suite with its Cool Blue theme, though. It claimed convention social highlight honours. Hockey player Tie Domi and *Canadian Idol* host Ben Mulroney, son of the former prime minister, schmoozed the room in the historic Hotel Godin, posing for pictures with partygoers. When Stronach showed up on the arm of Peter MacKay, she waved off an extended microphone. There was no way she was going to ruin a perfectly good party with a speech. Down below on a caged-in dance floor, the place was rocking hard to a light show from hundreds of battery-powered, flashing ice cubes, which had been placed in fruity martinis. *National Post* writer Siri Agrell stuck a pair down her bra to interesting effect, mostly on males. Ottawa's CanWest bureau production editor Rhonda Cunning was dancing up a storm with her back to the stage when the two-man band unleashed the 1980s hit "Life Is a Highway."

"Isn't this a great cover of Tom Cochrane?" she yelled to no one in particular. Someone suggested she turn around. "That IS Tom Cochrane," they said. She still hasn't lived that one down.

Only Belinda Stronach would fork over $86,000 for a policy convention hospitality suite featuring a Canadian musical icon. And only in her orbit could rumours circulate that Bruce Springsteen was going to show up—and be taken seriously enough for fans to gather on the street outside.

The Conservatives and Belinda Stronach were Cool Blue all right. But things were going to get red hot very quickly.

— NINE —

INTO THE
WOODSHED

IT STARTED FALLING APART on her 38th birthday. As she walked into a rare evening meeting of the 99-member Conservative caucus on Monday, May 2, an outstretched tape recorder gave Belinda Stronach an idea that, it can be said almost without exaggeration, changed the course of Canadian political history. Her colleagues were salivating to force a second election in as many years at the earliest possible opportunity, but Stronach was vehemently against defeating key provisions of the amended budget her party planned to use to topple the government. Perhaps, she figured, a national newspaper headline would make Conservative Leader Stephen Harper have second thoughts.

Any notion of voting down the Liberal government's budget in a confidence vote was a bad idea, she told *Globe and Mail* Ottawa bureau chief Brian Laghi. It could backfire against the party, delay worthwhile funding for cities and hand the Bloc Québécois more seats.

"I do have a concern that the voting against the entire budget will impact negatively in my riding," she said. "We can't jeopardize the funding for the infrastructure programs, which include transportation roads and public transit."

Inside the caucus meeting, as Harper went through the motions of soliciting MPs' views on the election force, Stronach made a rare statement to the caucus. She usually sat there in silence, wincing if the debate got too loud or right wing for her tastes. While sensing the tide was coursing against her, she had cautioned MPs a local poll in her riding showed 80 percent of her constituents opposed an early election call. *So what?* a few MPs scoffed in response. The public never supports an election in opinion polling. It doesn't mean they'll vote against the party for causing it. The caucus chair then called for a show of hands. Support went overwhelmingly in favour of the early election. Harper stood at the podium to send them off with a pep talk and a warning: Prepare for a June campaign and stick to the party line. He then waded into a waiting scrum to tell reporters his party's support for toppling the government later that month was "unanimous."

Back in her office, Stronach watched the coverage of Harper's exit and wondered how the leader's declaration would play against her public musings.

The next day's front-page headline—"Stronach sees risk in forcing fast election"—shot an off-script message at Harper with a bullet. Inside the Opposition leader's office, aides gasped and shook their heads knowing a line had been crossed by their leader's least favourite MP. It could not go unnoticed. And it would certainly have to be challenged. A summons arrived at Stronach's office around noon, ordering her to report to Harper's suite immediately after Question Period wrapped up at 3 PM It was not just highly unusual; it was unprecedented. Stronach had never been called by the leader's office before on any issue.

"I think I'm in trouble," she told her staff as she headed for the Centre Block.

THE ORNATELY CARVED ceilings and walls of the fourth floor Official Opposition leader's suite are arguably more upscale than the prime minister's office one floor below. That's because it was built to be the Centre Block PMO until John Diefenbaker refused to leave after his defeat. Lester Pearson simply moved prime ministerial operations to the third floor, where it has remained ever since. Ornate or not, Stronach dreaded entering the office and Harper wasted no time before launching into a thorough dressing down of his International Trade critic in front of House Leader Jay Hill and Caucus Whip Rob Nicholson.

"Don't you ever do that to me again," Harper warned, barely containing his notorious temper, the veins on his neck bulging while her fellow MPs studied the floor in obvious embarrassment.

Stronach protested she'd given her comment to Laghi before any caucus gag order had been imposed. Besides, she argued, supporting elements of the budget was merely acting on behalf of her constituents. A few days earlier she'd met with the York regional chair Bill Fisch and the last thing he'd told her was how desperately the infrastructure money in the proposed budget was needed to cope with the region's population growth. She'd pledged to help him get it.

Harper impatiently waved her off with the back of his hand, telling her to stop causing trouble and undermining his leadership. She should forget about becoming the Conservative leader, he warned, and he would do everything to prevent it. Stronach pushed back, saying she felt underutilized in the party and offered to take a more constructive role in helping the party as a team player.

"I told Stephen Harper, 'If I wanted to knife you in the back, I could've done that hundreds of times, but I want to remain a team player.'" Others in the meeting recall tempers were frayed and that Stronach recoiled at an experience totally foreign to her.

"There's no doubt Stephen was very, very angry," recalls one witness.

Harper tersely terminated the meeting. It was over in 10 minutes.

"He just couldn't get over thinking it was the leadership he thought I wanted," she says. "He took it very personally that I ran against him. You should be able to turn the page. Tony Clement and I turned the page for the greater good of the party and the country. He never did that. Watch his leadership if he goes forward because you can't be a one-man show and run the country. It's going to be very interesting to see his style."

Stronach returned to her office frustrated but not visibly flustered.

"He just doesn't get it," she told her curious staff. "It's very disappointing."

It was hostile enough to convince Stronach she would be forever outside the loop as long as this leader was in charge. Standing with the Liberals and the New Democrats to support the budget amendment, even if it meant sitting as an independent MP, suddenly crossed her mind. Knowing the horrific price that would carry under Harper's heavy-handed rule, leaving politics seemed almost appealing.

BELINDA STRONACH WAS the star attraction a few hours later at a dinner convened by Rod Love, the former Ralph Klein chief of staff who had supervised the Alberta leg of Stronach's Conservative Party leadership bid a year earlier. An eclectic group of former Klein aides, government lobbyists and columnists gathered at the Bravo Bravo restaurant on Ottawa's Elgin Street to drink many litres of red wine and scarf down some decent, if unremarkable, Italian food. Stronach was the last to show.

Love placed the guest of honour at his left side and ordered another litre of red. Stronach demurred, saying she'd prefer sparkling water. Eyebrows around the table raised a bit. Stronach isn't one to shy away from a glass of wine or three, a batch of vodka crantinis or, on rare occasions, a shooter bar. For someone with a notoriously ravenous appetite, she wasn't very hungry either and ordered a plain salad without dressing, picked away at it and said little while the rest of the table wolfed down bowls of steaming pasta to increasingly loud and loquacious conversation.

I ribbed her about the sudden personality change and asked the quiet soda-sipper for ID to prove she was, in fact, the former fun-loving Belinda Stronach. She shrugged.

"Sorry, but I got taken to the woodshed today," she said. "Stephen isn't very happy with me."

She wouldn't elaborate, but it wasn't necessary. The reason was as clear as the headline beaming out from every *Globe and Mail* newspaper box.

Stronach returned to her hotel with a Pez candy dispenser as a gift for Deputy Leader Peter MacKay, who now shared her bed most nights. She told MacKay about her meeting with Harper and her increasing discomfort with the Conservative Party. MacKay sympathized with her plight, but urged her to stick it out. *Typical*, an irritated Stronach thought to herself. She was increasingly fed up with fellow MPS who leaned one way in private talks with her and another in front of the leader or his cronies. Peter MacKay was becoming just as two-faced as they were, she thought. He goes with the flow, satisfied with merely waiting for an opportunity to arise. Stronach, on the other hand, saw herself as someone aggressively challenging unpleasant realities and embracing change whenever it's required.

Still, there was no hint Stronach was less than two weeks from a remarkable change. She took a trip to Montana with Conservative Agriculture Critic Diane Finley to raise Canadian concerns about a rogue Montana judge who had granted a temporary injunction against reopening the border to Canadian cattle after an outbreak of bovine spongiform encephalopathy (BSE) in two Alberta cows.

"If Paul Martin is too distracted by his own political misfortune to govern, we will continue to step up to the plate," she told reporters. "Someone must defend the interest of hard-working and suffering Canadian ranchers."

It didn't sound like someone rehearsing for a Liberal Cabinet position.

But small issues were becoming last straws for Stronach. As a billionaire's daughter, she is not accustomed to rejection and humiliation. She had been denied a legitimate speaking role on stage at the recent party policy convention, and a pre-election television campaign had been built around a handful of star MPs and she wasn't one of them. At the Ontario caucus meeting the day after the Harper showdown, she stoically listened as eastern Ontario MP Gordon O'Connor, a retired army general and future Defence minister, lambasted MPs who dared embarrass their leader with divergent views. He never mentioned Stronach by name, but nobody missed the target. The same day she submitted a legislative analysis on a private members' initiative called the Taiwan Affairs Act, which was brought to the Commons floor by B.C. MP Jim Abbott. The bill proposed to restore diplomatic relations with the breakaway Chinese province and recognize it as an official trading partner. Stronach had been horrified by the prospect of the act passing, and wrote a lengthy warning about the economic risks and implications of infuriating the Chinese economic tiger. Foreign Affairs Critic Stockwell Day wrote a contrary view, arguing the recognition of Taiwan was long overdue. Yet when it came time to debate the merits of supporting or opposing the legislation in caucus, Harper cut off Stronach before she could deliver her report. It would be a free vote, he ruled, and moved on to the next item. Stronach sat down and seethed.

Two days later, her malaise deepening into a full-fledged funk, Stronach adjourned to a cafeteria three floors above the Commons with her aide, Mark Entwistle. The pair sipped their tea and coffee without saying much until Entwistle finally broke the silence.

"Belinda, you've got to be questioning whether you're in the right home," he said.

Stronach was surprised it was that obvious and equally shocked at how much she agreed with the observation. It was an epiphany of sorts for the rookie MP. Her days as a Conservative MP were now officially numbered, she decided. Voting against the Liberal budget was no longer an option.

Screw Stephen Harper. She'd show him.

TEN

THE REJECTION
DEFECTION

WITH A WEEK TO GO before the budget vote, a brooding Stronach attended the $1,000-per-plate Woodrow Wilson Foundation awards dinner at Toronto's Liberty Grand, where grocery store magnate Galen Weston and former Ontario Premier Bill Davis were being honoured for their business and political accomplishments. The guest list was long and blue chip. Power Corp's Paul Desmarais, Barrick Gold's Peter Munk and assorted bank presidents circled the room. Schmoozing the crowd with long-time friend George Marsland in tow, Stronach bumped into former Ontario Premier David Peterson and his wife, Shelley.

Peterson first met Stronach in Switzerland when she was in her early 20s. He'd taken a break from a political trade mission in Davos to go skiing with Frank Stronach, and his daughter, an expert skier, had tagged along. They'd kept in touch ever since, running into each other at the same parties or fundraisers and occasionally visiting each other's homes. He recalls inviting her up to his horse farm in Caledon where Stronach had noted that the groom's children, who were slightly younger than her own kids, seemed a tad threadbare in the fashion department. She asked Peterson if the family would object to receiving her kids' hand-me-downs, most of them barely worn through one season.

"That's how my groom's kids suddenly became the best-dressed students in their school," Peterson grins. "And it wasn't just a one-off thing. Boxes kept arriving once or twice a year with the best clothes you can imagine."

The two chatted briefly in the hubbub of the ritzy cock-tail party. Peterson made small talk and asked how Stronach was doing, expecting the standard "fine" by way of response. Not so this time. Stronach told him she wasn't happy under Harper's leadership politically and was at a "crossroads" per-sonally. She sounded lost, adrift and uncharacteristically depressed, nothing like the life-of-the-party friend he knew. Peterson sympathized, gave her a hug and moved on, but left the event that evening perplexed at Stronach's comments. Here was a Conservative leadership candidate who'd run as an MP under Harper less than a year ago and was now dating the deputy leader of the party, and yet Peterson got the dis-tinct impression she was signalling her interest in becoming a Liberal. It didn't make sense. Too incredible to believe. He let it slide.

The phone rang the next morning with Stronach on the line. She was preparing to leave for Ottawa to attend a can-didates' school for Conservatives, gearing up for what seemed like an imminent election. She wanted to talk options to deal with her "dilemma" on the upcoming vote. Quitting was a possibility. Sitting as an independent and voting with the government to support the budget was another. Or, if vivid imaginations were stretched here, she could become a Liberal.

Peterson tried to talk her out of quitting and asked her to start thinking seriously of crossing the floor. But before things got carried away, he decided to seek clearance from the top to start reeling Stronach in from the cold. He called Tim Murphy, then chief of staff to Prime Minister Paul Martin.

The balding, bespectacled Murphy is a former Liberal MPP in Ontario, and was a senior aide in Peterson's own majority government in the late 1980s. He is schooled and shrewd in the ways of political skullduggery, and held considerable sway over a prime minister often seen as malleable. Murphy listened to Peterson's defection suggestion with considerable skepticism. Others had made similar overtures to the government, and Murphy was about to become implicated in the Gurmant Grewal affair, a B.C. Conservative MP who had secretly taped talks with Liberals. The tapes seemed to suggest Grewal would receive a payback—Murphy had hinted at a "nice comfy fur" welcome mat—if he crossed the floor to support the government. The last thing Murphy wanted was another botched defection and this seemed too preposterous to be possible. Conservative star Belinda Stronach! Becoming a Liberal? Inexplicable.

Peterson insisted Stronach seemed serious about wanting a divorce from the Conservative leadership. She was feeling underutilized by the party, ignored by a hostile leader, and was about to be force-marched into a campaign she opposed on multiple levels. It added up to *something* profound.

"So what should I do?" Peterson asked.

"Okay, go ahead," Murphy said, shaking his head. "But I'm not going to spend a lot of time hoping it's true."

Three hours later Peterson called back after talking again to Stronach.

"It's real," he said. "She's either coming over or getting out of politics altogether."

The time had come, Murphy decided, to alert the prime minister to this bizarre recruiting possibility. Contacted at his farm in western Quebec, Martin didn't take it seriously either, but told Murphy to let things move along without dangling a Cabinet carrot. At least not yet.

AT THIS POINT, Stronach decided to consult her most reliable oracle. Frank Stronach. She poured out a tale of woe of how Harper had warned her she'd never be the party leader and accused her of not being a team player.

"I know we talked one or two days before and she said she was really unhappy and that she couldn't be on the same wavelength as Harper," Stronach recalls. "I just said, 'Follow your heart.' Keep in mind we don't need anything from anyone. We are international and Magna does $23 billion now with over a billion cash in the bank."

Belinda Stronach told her father she wasn't prepared to run back to the money just yet. She had another option. She just had to make sure it was the right one. The confirmation wasn't long in coming.

That Friday afternoon Stronach returned to Ottawa, along with Conservative candidates who had flown in from across Canada for a pre-election orientation session. Stronach had been told she would be put on display, but not allowed to speak at the event. On Saturday morning she arrived for candidates' school with fellow MP Lee Richardson of Calgary slightly late for a training session featuring Tom Flanagan, the shadowy former academic from the University of Calgary and top adviser to Harper. He was lecturing the new recruits on the dos and don'ts of effective campaigning and was showing off a few examples of negatives. One of them was a blown-up photo of Belinda Stronach being interviewed by reporters. In the background was the infamous picture of Robert Stanfield dropping the football as the defining image of the 1972 federal election campaign. *Be aware of embarrassing optics like this*, a panelist stressed. Heads turned to grin at Stronach at the back of the room.

"I thought it was unnecessary," Stronach recalls. "If you're trying to build a team and be respectful of human beings, that's not how you go about it. It was disappointing."

Ironically, at least one Conservative observer was worried enough about her dark mood to begin telegraphing his concern through back channels. Strategist Jaime Watt, who had helped Stronach's leadership bid, had run into her at the dinner and recalls she was "trembling" as she discussed her encounter with the leader. The next day Watt went upstairs in Navigator Strategies, his Toronto communications company, to talk with associate Patrick Muttart, who had close contacts inside Stephen Harper's office.

"I couldn't understand why she was being treated this way and why she'd been left out of the advertising campaign they were putting on television," remarked Watt. "She's the only one who can draw a crowd."

Watt suggested Muttart send a quiet alert to Harper's office that the party had a very alienated MP on its hands. Muttart, he recalls, didn't seem particularly concerned.

BACK ON THE PHONE lines, Peterson started angling for a suitable reward to land such a big catch for the government.

"She's not coming across to sit as a backbencher," he told Murphy.

A mini-Cabinet shakeup triggered by Toronto MP Judy Sgro, having been punted from her Citizenship and Immigration post during an ethics probe into Romanian strippers being fast-tracked into Canada, had temporarily parked Human Resources and Skills Development responsibilities under Intergovernmental Affairs Minister Lucienne Robillard. That, Peterson told Murphy, would be the perfect parachute landing for his friend Belinda. Ironically, the only person he had to convince was Stronach herself.

"What the hell's Human Resources about anyway?" Stronach asked after Peterson briefed her on his Cabinet suggestion.

Only after learning it included responsibility for the labour market, employment insurance and lifelong learning, areas closely aligned to her business interests, did Stronach find the idea attractive. But she insisted on a democratic reform role after reading a column by veteran *Toronto Star* columnist Jim

Travers and bouncing ideas off her pal George Marsland, a fast-talking gay activist who served as Frank Stronach's executive assistant and worked with Belinda Stronach on the Magna essay-writing contest.

When Marsland first heard Stronach was negotiating a floor-crossing, he suggested she sit as an independent MP to avoid being viewed as crass and opportunistic. Stronach dug in her heels.

"There's a window here. I want to take responsibility for making something change for the better," Marsland quotes her as saying.

In fact, he says now, Stronach was prepared to walk away from the Liberals if their offer was confined to the Ministry of Human Resources, a version of events that clashes with the PMO story.

"Her first role and primary goal was to be the first person in Canadian history to be a minister of democratic reform. The deal would not hold without it. She was prepared to walk away," Marsland says.

But Peterson insisted she needed to have a full ministry to be taken seriously. And while he was at the negotiating table, he insisted she have a seat on the secretive Operations Committee, which serves as air traffic control for decisions flying between ministries and Cabinet under the careful eyes of Deputy Prime Minister Anne McLellan.

"That way you'll always be in the loop," he said.

It was music to Stronach's ears.

Increasingly daunted by Peterson's lengthening list of defection demands, Murphy says he finally insisted on a face-to-face meeting with Stronach.

"Until I meet her, I'm not negotiating," he said. "Once I know she's crossed, then we'll talk arrangements."

Peterson booked a room at the Château Laurier and flew up Monday morning. The deal would be sealed there at 4 PM, but a cone of silence had to come down over the talks.

"The minute it goes public, everybody loses flexibility to manoeuvre and pull back from it," Murphy warned.

WHEN HE ENTERED the suite to see Belinda Stronach seated between Mark Entwistle and David Peterson, Tim Murphy had a disbelieving giddy look on his face. While the defection was discussed with Peterson on the phone, it had somehow seemed too abstract to be real. But seeing Stronach was believing that Parliament's most glamorous MP, a Conservative trophy of mainstream moderation, was ready and willing to become a Liberal on the eve of a confidence vote the government was doomed to lose. Murphy summoned an equally incredulous PMO communications director Scott Reid to the hotel room to map out the defection process and media strategy.

"This is a huge thing I'm doing," Stronach told both men after signing off on the Cabinet and committee appointments. "It has a lot of implications and a number of people will be profoundly disappointed in me. I've got to sit with Paul [Martin] and have a chat and look him in the eyes and make sure we share the same values."

Murphy thought it sounded corny, but agreed and booked her for drinks with the prime minister three hours later.

WORD WAS ALLOWED to seep out on a need-to-know basis. Party president Mike Eizinga was notified the Liberal seat count was about to increase by one very big name. Lucienne Robillard was advised she'd be relieved of Human Resources from her dual responsibilities. And Karl Littler, deputy chief of PMO staff, was dispatched to Newmarket where local lawyer Martha Hall Findlay was about to get some very bad news. Hall Findlay had gamely fought Stronach in the 2004 election as the Liberal candidate, finishing 689 votes shy of becoming a Conservative giant killer. She had just been acclaimed as a repeat Liberal challenger for the upcoming election when Littler called to request a private talk at a Liberal fundraiser she was attending. He wasn't allowed to let slip the reason for the chat lest everything fall apart at the negotiating table.

A few minutes before arriving at the fundraiser, Littler phoned for instructions. Was he free to tell Hall Findlay the reason she was being forced off the ballot? Murphy had Stronach's commitment in hand and gave him the go-ahead, but he was still nervous. He sensed Stronach hadn't grasped the significance of her decision. It seemed very important to her personally, but the political ramifications of a former Conservative leadership candidate crossing the floor while a Parliament was hanging in a precarious balance didn't seem to have sunk in. She didn't appear mentally braced for the outrage she was about to unleash and the grief she was about to cause herself. *Oh well*, he thought. No point in stressing out Stronach with his version of the ugly truth about her defection consequences.

Stronach had asked if she could give her closest Conservative mentors—former Prime Minister Brian

Mulroney and former Ontario Premier Bill Davis—advance notice of her move, but Murphy vetoed it until the next morning. He didn't want to risk either of them arm-twisting his turncoat into changing her mind. The meeting broke up at 5 PM.

Strange, Murphy thought. There'd been no mention of Peter MacKay.

STRONACH LEFT TO freshen up for the most awkward encounter among the many she'd had in the previous 72 hours. She had a 7 PM dinner date booked with the deputy leader of the party she was poised to leave and had to pretend nothing unusual was taking place. For 90 minutes she sat across from the third-term Nova Scotia MP, making small talk with her lover of 10 months with only occasional references to the volatile political landscape enveloping Ottawa. She recalls feeling intense guilt at staying mum over one dinner, while, unbeknownst to her, a welcome-aboard feast of venison was being prepared a mile away by the chef at 24 Sussex Drive.

Stronach says there's a very good reason why she decided to keep such profound news a secret from MacKay. It was, she insists, for his own good; to protect him from a horrific conflict of interest. If she'd told MacKay of her plans, his deputy leader obligations would trump his personal entanglement in the affair, forcing him to alert Harper to this imminent political relations disaster. But it would cause Stronach considerable grief in terms of public views of who was the good, the bad and the ugly in the aftermath. The perception

With father Frank looking over her shoulder, Belinda Stronach announces her intention to seek the Conservative Party leadership at Aurora Legion Hall on January 20, 2004. Sixteen months later, she crossed the floor to become a Liberal cabinet minister. (CP Photo/Frank Gunn)

With Stephen Harper (right) and Tony Clement (middle) looking on, Belinda Stronach delivers her opening statement at the Conservative leadership candidate's debate in March 2004. She had refused to participate in earlier debates organized by national news networks. A few months later, Stronach gave Clement $100,000 to help reduce his campaign debt. (CP Photo/Ryan Remiorz)

Stronach was riding high in the saddle early in the campaign. Her first appearance in Calgary forced organizers to scramble to find a larger venue due to a huge demand for tickets to hear her speak. She took a break from the hustings to horse around a bit at a ranch in Cochrane, Alberta. (CP Photo/Jeff McIntosh)

Her fate as runner-up was already sealed by the time Stronach arrived in Toronto on the eve of the leadership convention aboard a campaign bus dubbed "The Belindamobile." The tour, which had received saturation coverage at the launch, was covered by only two reporters during the final days of the three-month campaign. (CP Photo/Adrian Wyld)

Belinda Stronach sits in the audience at the Conservative leadership convention with her parents after delivering her speech without a text—only a few cheat notes.

Stronach gives leadership campaign manager John Laschinger a peck on the cheek for his role in landing her second spot in the three-way race. (Tom Sandler)

Stronach with former boyfriend Peter MacKay in happier times. Her father, Frank, thought the pair was altar-bound until their acrimonious breakup the night before her defection to the Liberals. (CP Photo/Jacques Boissinot)

Stronach arrives at the Conservative policy convention on St. Patrick's Day 2005 with top aide Mike Liebrock. She was quietly backed by a team of hired guns monitoring debates and decisions to keep her from being caught unaware by convention developments. (Peter Bregg/*Maclean's*)

Belinda Stronach, pictured here with Calgary MP Lee Richardson, bid $2,000 for this Spongebob Squarepants doll at a children's charity fundraiser in 2005. She planned to take the stuffed toy, a television cartoon character rumoured to be gay, to a Conservative caucus meeting as a humorous protest of her party's opposition to same-sex marriage. A few weeks later, she joined the Liberals. (Don Martin)

Defection day. After a sleepless night, Belinda Stronach arrives with Prime Minister Paul Martin to gasps from photographers waiting outside the National Press Building in Ottawa on May 17, 2005. After reading a statement explaining her reasons for leaving the Conservatives to become a Liberal cabinet minister, she shook Martin's hand before wading into a throng of media. Twelve hours later, she flew home to deal with shocked staff in her Aurora constituency office. (CP Photo/Tom Hanson)

(CP Photo/Jonathan Hayward)

Two days later, newly appointed Human Resources Minister Belinda Stronach is surrounded by reporters after helping the Liberal minority government win a confidence vote, May 19, 2005. (CP Photo/Ryan Remiorz)

Stronach arrives at her first Liberal caucus meeting and is given a standing ovation from MPs grateful for her help in averting a federal election. (CP Photo/Tom Hanson)

It was no cliffhanger on January 23, 2006 when Stronach flattened her Conservative challenger in a federal election. She took the stage with campaign manager Kyle Peterson and father, Frank Stronach. The reserved smiles underline the fact her Liberal party lost government and she lost a Cabinet job that night. (Tom Sandler)

Stronach calls American economist Jeffrey Sachs her mentor for his humanitarian work helping the African poor become self-sufficient. She accompanied the founder of the Millennium Village concept on a ten-day tour to four African nations in the summer of 2005 with comedian Rick Mercer.

Stronach says fighting poverty in Africa will remain a personal priority during and after her political career. She plans to return to Africa in early 2007 to deliver vaccines and climb Mount Kilimanjaro as part of a charity fundraiser.

(George Whiteside, georgewhiteside.com)

of Belinda as a political two-timer, scheming for personal advancement even during a last supper with her unsuspecting boyfriend, would quickly take hold. In the battle for public empathy, MacKay would be seen as the dumped victim, Stronach the duplicitous villain. The truth was another story.

AFTER GREETING HER at the front door of 24 Sussex Drive, Paul Martin tried to pretend it was just a routine matter as he served up tea and coffee in the sunroom with Murphy, Entwistle and Stronach. He didn't directly approach the matter of her floor-crossing at first, talking in more abstract terms about the challenges of the Liberal Party, and matter-of-factly about the stress and strains of being in government. Finally, he could contain himself no longer.

"Holy shit, Belinda. You surprised me with the floor-crossing," said Martin, as he invited Stronach to join him for her second dinner of the evening.

Then the prime minister giggled like a schoolboy. He knew how to count. The prospect of an election had faded dramatically that night.

STRONACH RETURNED TO her hotel suite at 11 PM, girding herself for confrontation. There was no delaying it any longer—MacKay had to be told his girlfriend was going over the fence and not coming back. She tried to be gentle—repeating her reasons for being unhappy and discussing the options she'd considered. Then she dropped the bomb. MacKay's reaction was volcanic fury. After an hour of listening to his diatribe about broken loyalties and betrayed love, Stronach called Entwistle.

"Peter's reacting very badly," she said in a quivering voice. "I'm going to talk to him again. I'll call you in the morning."

Entwistle didn't know morning meant 4 AM, when Stronach called again to say it wasn't getting any better and that she thought the defection might have to be cancelled or delayed. MacKay, the fair-haired boy of a family with deep Conservative roots, was in full-frontal partisan assault. Stronach phoned her father, who said it was his daughter's decision and urged her to follow her heart. Others insist Frank Stronach wholeheartedly backed her Liberal ambitions, which was true enough, and there are even taxi drivers in Ottawa who swear he was driven and picked up from 24 Sussex four nights before the defection, a rumour he denies.

"This will destroy the Conservative Party," MacKay shouted.

"I think the Conservative Party is a little stronger than one person," Stronach retorted.

And so it went on until MacKay left for his apartment with Stronach crying in her room, their romance in ruins.

"Maybe I was naïve in some ways," Stronach says now. "I still think it's possible to see someone in an opposite party. Clearly, he didn't agree. I would've liked another day to talk him through it, to get him to understand what I was going to do and why."

Just before 8 AM Entwistle knocked on the door of her suite to find her with wet eyes, lined with dark bags from a sleepless night. He had written a statement, but Stronach didn't sound like she planned to read it. They talked for a few minutes before he left to meet Murphy and Reid, who were waiting to prep their prized recruit on the madness and media frenzy ahead.

"Um, we've got a problem," Entwistle told them.

Belinda was having second thoughts and might want to delay everything for another day. Murphy's face went white.

"It's too late to have a problem," he said. "We've vacated the Cabinet position, we've cleared the riding for her, and she's told the prime minister she's coming over. She can't go back now."

Entwistle slumped his shoulders.

"I'll go talk to her again."

The two men paced the suite, apoplectic at the thought of having to undo all the preparations and knowing it was only a matter of hours before the story of their botched defection would leak out to humiliate them and the party on the eve of a possible election. After 45 minutes, Entwistle returned.

"Whoa, that was close," he said with obvious relief. "I think we're okay."

Peter MacKay woke up alone, knowing he'd failed to stop the defection. There was nothing left to do but start alerting the party to the Stronach situation. His first call was to Stephen Harper. Then he called Brian Mulroney. Phone and e-mail traffic immediately picked up speed in senior Conservative circles as word fanned out across the capital.

Just after 8 AM, Stronach phoned confidant George Marsland, her mind finally made up but nervous about the fallout.

"Belinda, you're going to get the shit kicked out of you. Be prepared to be nationally pulverized over this," he recalls telling her. "But you're going to change the course of the government and be the first minister in history to have responsibility for the system."

She sounded reassured. They giggled before saying goodbye.

Just before 10 AM, John Waterfield of the Parliamentary Press Gallery hit the public address button in his office to announce Prime Minister Paul Martin would be hosting a news conference in half an hour in the national press theatre. Eyebrows raised and foreheads creased in news bureaus throughout the capital. Martin had rarely allowed himself to be grilled in the media-controlled domain, an issue of considerable friction between gallery members and PMO staff. To give reporters less than an hour's notice of a news conference amid so much political volatility put everyone on red alert for anything from a snap election call to a cabinet shuffle. Sources were hastily milked for information, but nobody was breathing a word about the prime minister's announcement. Curiosity levels spiked even higher amid such unusual secrecy, and reporters rushed into the theatre to stake out prime seats—the better to ask questions at what promised to be a major news event.

AT 10:20 AM, Stronach met David Peterson at the hotel's east entrance where the prime minister's motorcade would pick her up in five minutes.

"Scarf or no scarf?" she asked him.

"Wear the scarf," Peterson said.

Stronach smiled as she dialed Stephen Harper's number on her cellphone. A terse Harper was ready for the call. He told her he'd already been briefed on her defection by MacKay. He made no attempt to change her mind and offered no opinion on the move. The call lasted less than a minute. The prime minister's motorcade pulled up and Stronach hopped into the back seat with a beaming Martin beside her.

There was no turning back now.

SITTING IN THE second row of the press theatre, *National Post* columnist John Ivison's jaw dropped as he checked out the message that had sent his BlackBerry vibrating.

"They've got Belinda," he muttered in his thick Scottish accent.

Who's got Belinda? we wondered.

"The Liberals. That's what it says here," he declared, waving the device in the face of the disbelievers.

"Horseshit," someone said.

Outside on Wellington Street, the prime minister had just arrived and was grinning from ear to ear as he marched into the National Press Building and dashed into the privacy of a news conference waiting area. Disappearing right behind him was a blur of blonde hair atop a famous face wearing a sheepish grin. The dots took only a few seconds to connect before dozens of thumbs flew over BlackBerry keypads. Reporters were warning their editors that the news bombshell was set to explode right before their eyes.

"Stop the presses," I wrote to mine. "Belinda Stronach has gone Liberal."

A smirking Murphy and Reid stood off to one side, basking in the triumph of their shocking coup, as Martin emerged from the waiting area with Stronach in tow. They took their seats before reporters who sat in stunned silence at the political spectacle of it all. Both national news networks went live as Martin read his opening statement.

"I am very pleased to announce Ms. Stronach will cross the floor and has agreed to join the Cabinet as minister of Human Resources and Skills Development," Martin read. "In addition, she will assume responsibilities for democratic renewal and will help guide the implementation of the recommendations that flow from the Gomery Commission's final report. I am particularly proud to have her join us at this important time," Martin continued. "The significance of her decision is not that it necessarily alters the outcome of Thursday's vote. Indeed, the fact is that we still do not know—"

He was interrupted by a precedent no parliamentary correspondent can recall having been set before. The media laughed out loud at a Canadian prime minister.

"Now wait a minute. Just a minute," Martin said, a you-got-me grin creasing his face. "We still do not know if the budget will pass or not...."

The laughter got louder still. Martin surrendered to the folly of his own pretence.

"Well, I gotta tell you, I can count. But the significance is that on Thursday, members of Parliament will stand and will be counted in the most watched vote of the last 25 years, and Belinda Stronach has chosen to stand for what she believes is best for Canada. That is gutsy. And that's why I'm proud to have Belinda Stronach as part of my team."

Give her credit. Gutsy it was. The best Stronach could deliver through her defection was a tie vote, which would then have to be broken by the Speaker. But if Independent MP Chuck Cadman decided to support the Conservatives, the reincarnation of the Alliance Party he had represented before the 2004 election, the Liberals would still be toppled into an election. There was a very real possibility Stronach's lifespan in Cabinet would be measured in hours.

"I cannot exaggerate how hard this was for me," Stronach said when it was her turn to speak, never taking her eyes off the text on the table before her. "The political crisis affecting Canada is too risky and dangerous for blind partisanship. The country must come first...."

Then she took a curious segue. She had to make this personal. It was about Harper, not the party.

"To have healthy politics in Canada, we need the checks and balances of more than one strong and vibrant party. Over time, the Conservative Party will mature and grow to provide that option. There are many good and talented folks I have a great deal of respect for in the Conservative Party, but I find myself at the crossroads forced upon me by the decision of the leader of the Conservative Party to try and force the defeat of this government this Thursday. I've been uncomfortable for some time with the direction the leader of the Conservative Party has been taking. I tried to play a constructive role within the Conservative Party to advance issues that really matter to Canadians in cities, to women, to young people, to many Ontarians. I regret to say I do not believe the party leader is truly sensitive to the needs of each part of the country, and just how big and complex Canada is."

The floor erupted with questions. When had she decided to defect? What did she mean by Harper's leadership was shallow? Why'd she sell out for a Cabinet job instead of sitting as an independent or backbencher? And, inevitably, what about the boyfriend? To that, and in sharp contrast to MacKay's future comments, Stronach's jaw tightened and she responded without the slightest hint of emotion.

"I have a great deal of respect for Peter MacKay and the integrity he has and the contribution he has made to the Conservative Party."

So was the romance on or off?

"My future relationship with Mr. MacKay is a private and personal matter which I will not comment on."

There was an instant fury across the land. Stronach received death threats, which were taken seriously by the RCMP. Security guards were deployed to watch her two children at their private school. A bitter Conservative MP sent out a mass e-mail containing her private BlackBerry address and urged people to bombard it with outrage, which quickly crashed the device. Her riding president, Stephen Somerville, called it a "stunning hypocrisy." Harper took blustery exception to her comment on his leadership about not understanding Canada's complexity.

"I never noticed complexity to be Belinda's strong suit," he noted dryly. He insisted the decision had not come as a surprise. "I had, unfortunately, come to the conclusion that

Belinda Stronach's sole ambition in the party was the leadership. Obviously, it will be interesting to watch her progress in the Liberal Party."

A distraught, sleep-deprived Peter MacKay took a fellow MP's advice and boarded a plane for Halifax to escape the limelight. The next day he welcomed satellite trucks to his father's potato patch for a carefully staged photo op for the newspapers. Reaction was mixed. Many women melted at the sight of a man suffering such heartsick anguish; others laughed it off as a shameless act of self-promotion.

Stronach watched MacKay's tearjerker, delivered in a hoarse whisper, with dismay and some disgust. Why was he making this so public? To her mind, she had been dumped by him, not the other way around. Why was everyone so fixated on the love story? Nobody was asking about her reasons for leaving. Her defection was, as one wag quipped, packaged into one tight headline: "Stronach robs Peter to pay Paul." It was the start of a very ugly breakup, one that would haunt her for months as MacKay's reaction manifested itself in snide comments, nasty e-mails and furious glares across the Commons aisle. For a woman who'd amicably divorced two men and still kept them as friends, Stronach found MacKay's bitter behaviour disturbing. There'd be no repairing this relationship, she decided.

STRONACH'S FIRST CALL as she left the press theatre was to her constituency office in Aurora. Then she called Brian Mulroney, Bill Davis and Mike Harris to discuss her reasons for leaving the Conservatives.

"I wish you hadn't done what you did," Mulroney said. "But this is a heavy decision. From a personal standpoint, I love you, Mila loves you and the family loves you."

On Bay Street, the Canadian dollar edged upward on the news of her defection, currency traders reacting positively to the reduced threat of a federal election. They could count too. An hour after the news conference, Stronach was ushered to Rideau Hall to take the oath of office and began a rotating series of media interviews along a lineup of satellite trucks surrounding the Governor General's residence. They were, for the most part, awful. Stronach stuck to lines that appeared to be implanted by microchip, not even listening to the question before blurting out a scripted response. Many CBC staffers rate theirs as one of the worst face-to-face interviews of all time as Stronach dodged and weaved questions from *The National*'s Peter Mansbridge.

"I remember doing the Mansbridge interview outside of Rideau Hall, and I was just fried by that point," she recalls ruefully. "I'd been outside for 45 minutes, I was freezing cold with only a light jacket on and I was just shivering. When you're fried and tired and cold, you make your mistakes. That was a mistake."

The Conservative caucus held an unscheduled meeting. Anger and frustration filled the room. Some exchanged whispers, wondering if a jealous and paranoid Harper had indeed driven her from caucus. Others argued it was the best thing that could've happened to a party ill-equipped to fight an election.

On May 19, Stronach stood behind her second-row desk to cast a critical vote for Bill C-48, the $4.8-billion federal budget amendment the united Conservatives and Bloc Québécois hoped would defeat the government. With the Liberals backing a budget supported by the New Democrats and independent MP Cadman, the confidence vote resulted in a 152–152 tie, broken in the government's favour by Speaker Peter Milliken, the Liberal MP for Kingston.

Outside the House of Commons, a grim-faced Stephen Harper said it was time for the Opposition parties to down tools. The brinkmanship, which had raged on Parliament Hill for a month, had to stop. The next push to take down the government would have to wait for the fall. A turncoat named Belinda had stopped everything.

LIBERAL POLITICIANS AND staff went wild in Ottawa's Studio 34 that night, mobbing Stronach like an electoral saviour as she elbowed her way through the packed nightclub. Tim Murphy pulled his prize recruit onto a small stage and urged Stronach to dance before the cheering throng. The disc jockey saw his shot and took it, slapping on Madonna's "Material Girl" just as Stronach started grooving to the music. Mortified by the words so many people equated with her lifestyle, Stronach quickly exited the stage. Within hours she was flying home to Aurora to be by her daughter's side. Nikki had been rushed to Toronto's Hospital for Sick Children for an emergency appendectomy. It may have been an omen of sorts. Her defection was hardly cause for Liberal celebration, though. Thanks to her, the Conservatives had just won the next federal election. They just didn't know it yet.

ELEVEN

PETER THE GRATE

W HOEVER DID THE Senate Chamber seating plan for the swearing-in ceremony of Governor General Michaëlle Jean on September 27, 2005 had a warped sense of humour. Seated at the table in the centre aisle reserved for Cabinet ministers was a solemn Belinda Stronach. Seated a few feet behind her in the regular MP spectator seats, framed perfectly to fit inside a television picture, was Peter MacKay, who was celebrating his 40th birthday that very day. Both fidgeted uncomfortably as the vice regal parade approached, acutely aware their close physical proximity had the tittering tongues around them wagging. Stronach finally decided someone had to break the ice. She'd heard about a party in Ottawa's market the night before, where national television icon Don Newman had served as master of ceremonies at a bash to celebrate MacKay's middle-age milestone. She turned around in her chair and congratulated him. MacKay trained his steely blue eyes on the former love of his life.

"How," he snarled, "can you live with yourself?"

That's the way it had been ever since her cool blonde shrug and his potato patch sniffle scripted a bona fide parliamentary soap opera in the aftermath of Stronach's high-stakes floor-crossing. Reporters recall MacKay breaking down in tears in Darcy McGee's pub on Sparks Street in Ottawa a few days after his Stronach relationship went terminal. Friends say he was inconsolable for months, his bitterness deepening instead of easing. He deliberately and defiantly wore a tie she'd given him only a few weeks earlier to the budget confidence vote, waving it slightly as she stood in her second-row Liberal seat, voting to keep the government alive. In the weeks that followed, MacKay's furious glares across the centre aisle so unnerved Stronach that her new colleagues decided to relocate her seat to another side of the Commons where direct eye contact was more difficult. MacKay's pain could not be contained. He spent hours commiserating with drinking pals and called Stronach's closest friend to give his side of the story. He sent Stronach bitter personal e-mails. Finally, seemingly having accepted the inevitable, he visited her children, bringing gifts and gently confiding he'd miss them terribly, but wouldn't be seeing them as much any more.

IF YOU STUDY MacKay's history, perhaps his fierce overreaction was not surprising. A partisan streak runs deep in his genes as the son of Elmer MacKay, the shrewd Brian Mulroney Cabinet minister and Atlantic Canada godfather who lost his marriage to long-distance commutes and political pursuits. To the MacKay way of thinking, the party triumphs over all other considerations. When a hot-blooded romance is up against cold-hearted politics, the MacKays' veins course with ice. And he believes there's a special place in hell reserved for those who sacrifice their Conservative Party loyalty on the altar of personal expediency.

When former Progressive Conservative leadership contender Scott Brison crossed the floor to join Paul Martin's Liberals in December 2003, it was MacKay whose contempt seethed with the most venom. He labelled Brison a hypocrite for putting political ambition ahead of principle, taking it personally because he alleged Brison had repeatedly confided he would never defect.

"I would rather know where people are and be able to see them in front of me on the Opposition bench than have them sneak up behind me," MacKay fumed in the aftermath. "I can't find any principle whatsoever in what's happened today."

He was still venting six months later while campaigning hard in an unsuccessful attempt to help the Conservatives unseat Brison in the riding of Kings–Hants.

"You know, crossing the floor, leaving the party at a critical juncture, I could never do that. I could never live with myself," he told a Halifax reporter. "It's just not in my nature to bail."

More than two years later, MacKay has yet to say a word to Brison except in the form of verbal shots across the Commons battlefield.

There are exceptions to MacKay's acute sensitivities, of course. If your name is David Emerson and you've bolted to his Conservative ranks in early 2006 for a Cabinet gig just two weeks after being re-elected as a Liberal MP in Vancouver, that's fine.

"He did so for altruistic reasons. No one can attribute the same nefarious motives here," insists MacKay.

But Stronach, she was different. That was "to salvage a government for a vote and get a Cabinet post," he argues.

Well, okay then....

PETER GORDON MACKAY was born on September 27, 1965 in New Glasgow, Nova Scotia, the region his family had settled in the 19th century. His early memories were of attending a one-room schoolhouse in Lorne without running water. He recalls kids scorching their winter hats and gloves while trying to dry them over a woodstove and the frigid experience of using the washroom, which was an "outdoor two-seater that was tipped over every Halloween." Beyond that, it was a normal upbringing in small-town Nova Scotia as the son of the local MP until, when he was just eight years old, his parents divorced.

"Politics was very much a factor in our family's breakup," MacKay says now. "That was a very painful time."

He moved with his mother, Macha Delap, to Wolfville in the Annapolis Valley, where her family had settled to run a blueberry farm after emigrating from Belfast. He credits his mother as having the greatest impact on his life, a woman of intense community spirit and involvement in charities and international organizations. He didn't see much of his father, whose 20-year Commons career culminated in a variety of senior Cabinet portfolios during the Mulroney majorities, among them minister of Public Works and solicitor general. The son visited his father from time to time and briefly transferred to Ottawa's Carleton University to be closer to him.

"But I actually saw less of him then," MacKay recalls. "He was working all week and he went home every weekend."

After graduating from Acadia University, MacKay was called to the Bar in June 1991 and started a criminal and family law practice in New Glasgow. He worked briefly for German steel giant Thyssen Henschel in Kassell before returning to Pictou County as one of two Crown attorneys seconded to the Westray coal mine disaster investigation. There was little sign the father's political itch had spread to the son. He never joined the PC Youth Association or attended Tory conventions as a delegate, wary of a political career that had broken up his family. Any frustrations with a legal system that MacKay found increasingly lenient were taken out as a win-at-all-costs centre for the Pictou County Rugby Football Club, where he broke his nose repeatedly and smashed his shoulder badly in the relentless pursuit of victory. Only after a few years of watching criminals and young offenders getting off with slap-on-the-wrist sentences did MacKay contemplate entering politics. In 1997, at age 31, he made a "snap decision" to seek the Progressive Conservative nomination in the riding of Pictou–Antigonish–Guysborough. It was a headlines-grabber for unusual reasons. Before he won the contest, MacKay was called onto the carpet by the director of public prosecutions and warned he was about to be fired for violating a law that banned public servants in positions of confidence from seeking political office. MacKay voiced his disagreement loudly and publicly, vowing legal action against the "reign of terror" his boss had created in the office. Cynics at the time suggest his dismissal was the first sign of MacKay as a master self-promoter.

"Being fired was the last thing I wanted to happen," MacKay protested at the suggestion from local editorial writers that he was milking free publicity from losing the $42,000-a-year job. "Luckily, I don't have a family to support, but I spent a great deal of my own money on my nomination campaign."

In what was perhaps a glimpse of a future when MacKay's view of the world would always be filtered through a partisan prism, the candidate saw his dismissal as a political conspiracy.

"I mean, we're talking about my candidacy as a Progressive Conservative and we happen to have a Liberal government in Ottawa and a Liberal government in this province, so they're going to have to answer that; I don't know," he shrugged.

More than 2,000 Tories attended his nomination showdown, which had to be moved into the largest arena in the county to handle the crowd. Standing defiantly at the back were nine Crown attorneys, who had come from across the province to support their Ottawa-bound colleague. MacKay squeaked by with 1,008 votes to 894 for town councillor Danny MacLeod.

ON JUNE 2, 1997, with 72 percent of the riding's vote behind him, MacKay marched to Parliament Hill in his father's footsteps, one of 20 Conservative MPs sent to Ottawa from the general election. He was appointed House leader and Justice critic, and set out to bring law and order to the

Conservative agenda. He supported the death penalty, endorsed minimum mandatory sentencing and opposed same-sex marriages. Being a rookie member of the fourth party didn't create many opportunities to be heard over the gunfire being exchanged between Preston Manning's Reform Party and Jean Chrétien's Liberals. MacKay caused a brief ruckus when he vowed not to file his shotgun with the new firearms registry, but sold it instead. Those who wanted him to take a defiant stand against compulsory registration were not impressed by the flip-flop. Even so, he commanded respect for pulling no punches in attacking the Liberals during Question Period and for giving good quote to media, while his rugged good looks placed MacKay atop the annual poll of Parliament Hill staffers as the sexiest male MP. And while his future potential to be leader was never in doubt, MacKay showed stubborn loyalty to his leader, Joe Clark. When former party president Peter Van Loan, now a Conservative MP, approached MacKay in an alleged effort to unseat the incumbent leader, he went public with the plot.

Despite his reputation as a womanizer, MacKay regularly mused about wanting to settle down in a marriage with children.

"You know what would be a huge roadblock for me?" he asked in an interview before entering the Conservative leadership race. "Family."

But political ambition always wins over personal considerations. He entered the race to replace the retiring Joe Clark as the frontrunner against fellow MP Scott Brison, Calgary lawyer Jim Prentice and Saskatchewan farmer David Orchard. His opening statement at an Ottawa news conference in January 2003 would prove ironic in a year when his party would ultimately reunite with its western Canadian Alliance cousin.

"I can tell you right now, I am not the merger candidate," MacKay stated. "I am not interested in institutional mergers with other parties. I am interested in co-operation with persons in other parties."

It was a sleepy leadership race. MacKay played it safe, knowing victory was his unless he talked himself into trouble. His only eyebrow-raising attacker was Brison, who blasted MacKay as the "status quo candidate" to start a feud that rages still. The campaign culminated with a 14-hour showdown in Toronto on May 31, 2003 before 2,600 delegates. With voting about to begin on the fourth and final ballot and the race down to a two-way contest against Jim Prentice, MacKay inked what became known as the "deal with the devil," obtaining Orchard's support in exchange for a pledge to re-examine the North America Free Trade Agreement, an almost treasonous move given that NAFTA was a crowning jewel of Mulroney's Conservative administration. But the first line of the four-clause deal scribbled on a piece of paper above MacKay's signature read: "No merger, joint candidates with the Alliance." Behind the scenes, MacKay's people were already hard at work on ways to break his word.

JUST TWO WEEKS later, Belinda Stronach met with Harper and MacKay, and set up emissaries from both parties to negotiate the terms of reunification. Former Ontario Premier Bill

Davis, former Deputy Prime Minister Don Mazankowski and Tory House Leader Loyola Hearn would represent the Progressive Conservatives. MP Scott Reid, Senator Gerry St. Germaine and former Alberta MLA Ray Speaker, one of the founders of the Reform Party, would be negotiating for the Canadian Alliance. By November the deal was announced and MacKay was campaigning for members to support a merger he promised never to allow.

"I regret having to sign that agreement," he admitted. "I was hoping to win the leadership with enough support without making any agreements, absolutely. But let's not forget—I went into the leadership contest to win and I suggest to you that any candidate that was there, faced with a similar offer, would have done so."

On December 7, the day after the joint membership embraced reunification of the once-bitter rivals, chief electoral officer Jean-Pierre Kingsley paid a rare weekend trip to the office to register the birth of the Conservative Party of Canada. Watching from afar, Orchard denounced the new party as "conceived in betrayal and born in deception." For MacKay, going back on his word was an act of personal sacrifice driven by what he believed was political necessity. He would be hounded as a promise-breaker at home in Nova Scotia and heckled as a sellout in Ottawa. Whenever he rose to ask a question, Liberal benches would erupt with cries of "What about Orchard?" In the end, MacKay's leadership lasted only seven months. His only legacy was to orchestrate his party's demise, his only reward was public humiliation.

THE BRUISED AND battered MacKay couldn't bring himself to contest another fight to win the new Conservative leadership and opted to sit out a race ultimately won by Harper over Stronach. As time wore on, MacKay had felt increasingly isolated from the victorious Harper's inner circle, treatment many felt was unworthy of a party co-founder. He was given a low profile in party promotion campaigns and sidelined during the 2004 election, only to watch Liberals win ridings that he felt could've been won for the Conservatives with more help. He felt slightly queasy at Harper's bizarre antics and inexplicable strategies late in the 2004 campaign, which many believe may have cost the party enough seats to win a minority government. He was frustrated by Harper's attitude toward him, believing the new leader viewed his party co-founder as a future threat who had to be marginalized. He soon discovered he wasn't the only former leadership candidate who had been getting Harper's cold-shoulder shove out of the spotlight. Peter MacKay had found a political soulmate in Belinda Stronach.

HOW THE LINK sorts out between his head and his heart might require analysis on a professional couch, but some suggest persistent bachelor MacKay's roving relationships with women from political backgrounds are connected to his parents' breakup under the pressures of public service. In the late 1990s, MacKay had a serious relationship with nurse Maribeth Ryan, daughter of a former Prince Edward Island NDP leader. That live-together romance was still going on in Ottawa when he fell for Lisa Merrithew, a charismatic strategist from Halifax and daughter of a Mulroney Cabinet minister. For a while, Casanova MacKay juggled the two relationships, which put him on the parliamentary rumour mill as the guy with "a brunette in Ottawa and a blonde in Halifax." When Merrithew finally staked a solo claim on MacKay's affections, she immersed herself in helping his career and working on the PC leadership. Standing on stage with MacKay after he was crowned the last leader of the Progressive Conservative party, her hand in his with their arms raised high, Merrithew clearly telegraphed her status as MacKay's wife-in-waiting. From the back of the hall, the next woman to steal MacKay's heart, even while he was still professing his faithful devotion to Merrithew, was watching. In an unrelated matter with major ramifications to come, Belinda Stronach's second marriage was on the rocks.

THE FUTURE COUPLE first met at a fundraiser in early 1999 when Stronach was engaged to Olympic speed-skating champion Johann Koss. MacKay was still being ranked as the sexiest politician in the parliamentary precinct, but Stronach didn't pay particular notice. She thought highly of him as a politician. She was a key fundraiser for his leadership race, putting about $250,000 in his coffers. And while MacKay stopped short of publicly endorsing her Conservative leadership bid, he clearly signalled a preference for her over Alliance Leader Stephen Harper. With Johann Koss now officially a former husband following the couple's January 2004 divorce, the friendship between the two attractive 38-year-olds had obvious potential for some serious fireworks.

Curiously, Stronach doesn't remember their first date. But during or shortly after the 2004 federal election campaign, their electoral connection went electric. Staff in Stronach's Aurora riding office wondered if something was up after MacKay started showing an inordinate amount of personal interest in their boss's well-being after the election. He invited her constituency workers to mingle with his staff in Ottawa to learn the secrets to getting things done inside the federal bureaucracy.

It took a few months for news of the romance to leak beyond the chattering classes of Ottawa. They had been busted by gossips, who had seen them dining together in intimate restaurants, and there was occasional speculation about the affair in tattletale newspaper columns. But neither side confirmed the connection, and they took pains to make their relationship appear platonic by never arriving at or departing from events together. Yet throughout the fall of 2004, MacKay was spending most nights with Stronach in her hotel suite. He became an expert at sneaking out of the Château Laurier early in the morning, disguised behind sunglasses and wearing a baseball hat. It wasn't until *Vancouver Sun* columnist Barbara Yaffe caught MacKay in a weak moment in late January 2005 that things became official.

"Suffice it to say, I'm very happy and quite smitten. Belinda is just a terrific person and we're getting along famously," he told her, before biting down on his tongue. "I guess that's really all I would say about it...without first talking to Belinda about giving any kind of interview on our relationship."

Stronach was blindsided by his public disclosure, but thought it was "sweet" to hear MacKay talking about her that way. Contacted by Yaffe, she confirmed they had recently taken a holiday in the Bahamas: "We've known each other for a few years and have always had a lot of respect for one another and of late we've started dating. Maybe I should say, spending time together; dating is more of a teenaged word."

They quickly fell in love. True, there were whispers his feelings were more intense than hers and dark suspicions she was using the relationship to milk MacKay for his organization pending a future run for the leadership, but there was never serious doubt that strong feelings went both ways.

SHE WAS RELUCTANT to spend more time away from her children than the weekday demands of working in Ottawa, so instead of returning to his Nova Scotia riding, MacKay often gave up family visits and rugby games to be with her in Aurora. The couple didn't venture out into Toronto's social spotlight often, preferring leisurely dinners with friends. MacKay found himself becoming deeply attached to Stronach's children. Frank Jr., for example, remains a high school rugby fanatic thanks to MacKay's introduction to the game on the fields surrounding the family estates.

"It was a really great time in both their lives," sighs Bonnie Shore. "Peter was a terrific mentor and adviser. He was a real gentleman. He was lovely to the family and to her friends."

Sheila Pearce agrees: "He was amazing. He would always come here. They were a great couple and really, really loved each other."

If MacKay was smitten with Stronach, her family was clearly smitten with MacKay. Both of Stronach's former husbands talk glowingly of MacKay as a decent and caring companion for their ex-spouse and say they were sorry to see the relationship end. Stronach's father, Frank, has nothing but good things to say about a love affair he felt was altar-bound: "The relationship had a chance. I sensed when they were together, they were very happy. They were playful and always joking and laughing at the stories they told each other. As a father, I liked him because he was a nice fellow and decent guy and so I thought they'd be good together."

THINGS, OF COURSE, came to a spectacularly ugly end on May 17, 2005, amid Stronach's overnight disclosure and discussion of her plan to leave the Conservatives and cross the floor to sit as a Liberal Cabinet minister. Friend George Marsland recalls Stronach fretting as she prepared to join MacKay for a dinner prior to meeting with Prime Minister Paul Martin to seal her defection deal.

"What am I going to do about Peter?" she asked nervously.

Marsland was adamant. MacKay could not be told until the last possible minute because he would be expected, as the party's deputy leader, to inform Harper immediately.

"If you care for him, you can't make him make that choice because he'll be left in the party and you'll be gone," he warned.

Stronach took his advice, waiting until after midnight to lay the shocking news on an unsuspecting MacKay. Friends of MacKay's recall it differently. They say he asked her point-blank where she was going after their dinner. She fudged a response and, when she returned three hours later, he pressed her again. Again she was evasive, dodging his questions until he angrily and suspiciously demanded an explanation. Either way, their 10-month romance died in the hours that followed, but not without her brief flirtation with a last-minute change of heart to stick with the Conservatives.

"She was happy with Peter. But she was afraid that he would convince her otherwise, that he could persuade her not to do it," Frank Stronach told me. "She just felt in her heart this is the right thing to do." Her pleading phone call in the middle of the night jolted him awake and kept the family patriarch up for the rest of the night wondering what to tell his torn, traumatized daughter as she wrestled with her conscience. "It was agonizing. I really didn't want to convince her one way or the other because she's all grown up and must make up her own mind, even though in my mind and heart, I thought she did the right thing. If Harper is the kind of a person who hates her, who needs it?"

MacKay bolted the capital for Halifax the next morning to escape what he knew would be a media feeding frenzy as Stronach's ex-boyfriend. Harper stepped into the void to deal with reporters. It was the closest Canada had ever come to a royal de-coupling. Ironically, the Conservative leader seemed to finally find compassion for MacKay where there'd been only simmering tension before.

"I think Peter is taking this pretty hard, as you could imagine," the future prime minister told a news conference. "If she has such a high opinion of Peter MacKay, I would venture today after my discussion with him, she has an awfully tough way of conveying that to him."

Senator Marjory LeBreton recalls talking to MacKay after he landed in Halifax.

"That night after she defected, he was mostly concerned about the kids. I think that's a reflection of his childhood, the result of a broken home and being raised by his mother," she says.

MacKay's desire for heart-mending privacy on the family's sprawling farm in Lorne didn't last long. Reporters demanding comment were tipped the next day as to where to find their victim, right down to which potato patch at what time. Satellite trucks roared into position as MacKay posed with rubber boots resting on a shovel in freshly turned soil, his puffy sleepless eyes squinting toward the horizon, the perfect camera-friendly image of a lover scorned by political adultery.

"My head's clear," MacKay said in a raspy whisper, as a dog romped in the background, "but my heart's a little banged up. It tries your soul. It was a blow. I didn't see it coming."

He wished Stronach's children well, but couldn't contain himself in condemning their mother.

"Never turn your back on your friends and your family and your colleagues like this," he advised. "It's not the way you conduct yourself in an honourable fashion, I don't think."

It was a media encounter that divided Canadian public opinion with little or no middle ground. Some women melted at the sight of hurtin' puppy MacKay. Others laughed at what they considered an obvious media set-up. Men either felt his pain or, as I did, deemed it pathetic. CBC television personality Rick Mercer called it "the most humiliating thing I have ever witnessed." *National Post* writer Siri Agrell weighed in with a younger woman's viewpoint: "Peter MacKay looked like a snivelling little girl on TV. We've all been dumped, Peter, and you yourself unceremoniously gave the boot to a lovely young woman after falling into Ms. Stronach's evil clutches. The Conservative Cuckold needs to suck it up, stop his crying and exact revenge." Perhaps former girlfriend Maribeth Ryan, a mother of two children, gave *Maclean's* magazine the most devastatingly blunt insight into MacKay's reaction: "I do feel badly for Peter. But quite frankly, as someone who knows him well, I think he was more upset about his public humiliation than his relationship ending."

Stronach herself was utterly appalled by the spectacle and tried without success to contact MacKay to demand his discretion, if only to protect her kids.

"I didn't see it live on television, thank goodness. Why would you do that?" she wonders now. "I couldn't understand why he would bring it up. I didn't talk about the personal side at all, and yet you see satellite trucks show up at his house. I was very disappointed that he had to expose the personal side."

Behind the scenes in the privacy of her home and condo, Stronach was also in a heartsick meltdown over the doomed affair.

"It was an awful time. I'd never seen Belinda go through anything like that before. It was the worst thing I'd ever seen her go through," says Sheila Pearce.

The spectacle went global when Stronach and MacKay were christened CNN's Political Play of the Week. The television news network described Stronach as a wealthy femme fatale and Bill Clinton's "good friend."

"Stronach made a move that shocked the normally staid world of Canadian politics," reported Bill Schneider, who compared the affair to "a film noir—betrayal, dangerous liaisons, in an exotic and alluring locale" before adding incredulously: "Canada?"

MACKAY LEFT THE potato patch and returned to Ottawa the next day for the confidence-testing budget vote and received a sustained standing ovation from his caucus when he rose to ask a question. He had deliberately worn a striped silk tie that was a recent present from Stronach.

"It was just one of those spontaneous gifts," he told an observant reporter, "just like other spontaneous things that happened."

After Stronach's vote saved the government and the Opposition parties decided to wait for an opportunity in the fall to force an election, MacKay couldn't resist a final dig before returning to Nova Scotia.

"I think I'll go home and walk my dog," he fumed into microphones. "At least dogs are loyal."

By the May long weekend, the lovers' quarrel was on its way to The Rock. The Liberals desperately wanted to win a federal by-election in Newfoundland to replace deceased Liberal MP Lawrence O'Brien. If they retained the seat, they'd be assured of retaining power with help from the New Democrats. MacKay was summoned to campaign alongside Harper for the Conservatives. Stronach was tapped to join a partisan army to help the Liberal candidate, but she did a quick touchdown in Halifax hoping to negotiate a ceasefire with MacKay. He refused to take her call.

"That's how he felt he had to act," argues Shore. "His heart is good and he's a good man. Was his behaviour weird? Yeah, maybe. If you broke up with somebody you loved, couldn't you act weird? For sure you would."

Things settled down a few weeks later, and MacKay called Pearce to book a time to say goodbye to Stronach's children. For two hours he told her about his family connections with the Conservative Party and why he viewed Stronach's defection an act of fundamental disloyalty to a party at a critical time in its bid to form a government.

"I couldn't understand why he felt that way at first, but then I realized this was somebody who came from a political family," says Pearce. "Belinda is so not like that. She's a non-partisan person who does what she believes for her own moral reasons, not necessarily following party lines. He was never going to be able to accept it, and she couldn't back away from it for political reasons."

Time still hadn't healed MacKay's broken heart when the Commons reconvened in the fall. Curious eyes from the press gallery invariably turned to watch MacKay's graphic reactions whenever Stronach answered questions as a Liberal Cabinet minister. He could be counted on to glare, shake his head or snort in disgust at Stronach's rehearsed responses. It finally got too much for her seatmates.

"They actually moved me in the House because he would stare every day, and it made all my colleagues feel uncomfortable," she recalls.

On the home front, Stronach was receiving an alarming amount of hate mail from men who felt she had used and abused MacKay. Her chronic problem with stalkers, including one who managed to sneak into the family compound and knock on her door, was exacerbated by the backlash.

"Any guy across the country who had a tough time with a woman took it personally," she says. "My support among men went down. But my support among women went way up. Strange."

BY THE TIME the Liberals were forced into a November 2005 election campaign, MacKay was back in singles circuit circulation. With Mila Mulroney playing matchmaker, he started dating glamorous Sophie Desmarais of the wealthy Power Corp. family. It was a short-lived affair, but cemented his reputation as having a desire for rich blondes. Even as the campaign headed for a successful conclusion with a Conservative minority government, Stronach was still not far from MacKay's mind. He'd call Marjory LeBreton on the Harper campaign bus periodically to check on the status of swing ridings. Once the obvious list of vulnerable candidates was exhausted, he'd pause: "Dare I ask?" LeBreton didn't need clarification. Unfortunately, she'd say, Belinda Stronach looks in good shape to reclaim the Newmarket–Aurora riding for the evil Liberals. MacKay would sigh and head back onto the campaign trail.

THE BITTERNESS LINGERS still. The morning after the 2006 Junos ceremony in Halifax three months after Stronach was re-elected to sit on the Liberal Opposition benches and MacKay was elevated to Foreign Affairs minister, Stronach approached an old friend in a hotel restaurant. She didn't notice MacKay having breakfast with his sister at a nearby table until it was too late to avoid an awkward encounter.

"I said, 'Hello, how are you?'" she recalls. "He didn't say anything back."

A few weeks later, ironically on the one-year anniversary of her floor-crossing, Stronach found herself in a Commons elevator with MacKay and his officials. She again said hello. MacKay stood silently staring at the elevator buttons.

"We don't talk and we don't communicate. It's so unfortunate. I cared a lot about him," she sighs. "And I still do."

TWELVE

AFTERMATH

O THERS HAD GONE before her. Joe Peschisolido in 2002, Scott Brison in 2003, Keith Martin in 2004. All were Conservative or Alliance MPs who had jumped to join the Liberals. But they didn't rate a row of satellite trucks outside their floor-crossing ceremony at Rideau Hall. Or an emergency caucus meeting by their former party. Nobody commissioned a public opinion poll on the motives behind their decision. The loonie didn't move on currency markets because they switched party colours. Nor did they endure wave after wave of coast-to-coast condemnation. That was reserved exclusively for Belinda Stronach in 2005. Reaction was fierce, unforgiving—and definitely sexist.

Alberta Conservative MLA Tony Abbott declared that Stronach had "whored herself out for power." Ontario Conservative MPP Bob Runciman called her an "attractive dipstick." Conservative MP Maurice Vellacott said Stronach had "prostituted" herself to get the Cabinet gig, a theme echoed in a *Journal de Montréal* cartoon of Stronach as a hooker in netstockings, leaning on a parked car as a leering prime minister invited her inside.

The contrast would become even more jarring in the wake of Vancouver MP David Emerson's jump to the Conservative front bench just two weeks after being re-elected a Liberal in January 2006. Not a single reference to whoring or prostitution followed that electoral treason. No provincial or federal Conservatives protested the rank opportunism of someone seamlessly moving between the Cabinets of two rival parties without a trace of remorse. Peter MacKay argued Emerson had taken an honourable route to better represent his riding, even though it had just voted 43 percent for the Liberals and 18 percent for the Conservatives.

PARLIAMENT HILL'S WEST Block is not air-conditioned, and things get hot when meetings are crowded with angry politicians and senators letting off steam. On the afternoon of May 17, 2005, where Stronach crisis management was the only item on the agenda, the room was in stifling hyperventilation. There were off-colour jokes at Stronach's expense. There was bitter talk of revenge, loyalty oaths, greater unity and much sucking up to Stephen Harper. Stronach's friends in the caucus sat in sheepish silence, fearing to peep a word of protest against the obvious overreaction.

All day long Parliament Hill had vented—and it reverberated across the nation. Harper had predicted it would cost Stronach her Commons seat in the upcoming election.

"I know that a number of our caucus members are feeling quite devastated and quite betrayed by this," he said.

"I thought it had become obvious to Belinda that her leadership ambitions would not be reached in this party regardless of whether or not we won the next election. I thought that would mean trouble, and frankly I'm relieved that we've at least gone through this before an election, rather than during it."

"Stronach is a bit of a tourist in politics," argued Calgary Southeast MP Jason Kenney. "She realized her very obvious leadership ambitions weren't going to be realized in the Conservative Party."

The man who first attracted her political interest, former Reform Party Leader Preston Manning, called it a "setback."

"It's disappointing for Conservatives because they're trying to build this bigger, broader tent," Manning said. "They [the Conservatives] are attracting candidates at a stronger and faster rate in Ontario than they were before, but this sort of thing doesn't help."

Perhaps the most surprisingly vitriolic reaction came from Tony Clement, who had savaged Harper during the Conservative leadership race as someone building firewalls instead of bridges across the country. While not yet elected as a Conservative MP, he assailed Stronach from the sidelines as a "destabilizing influence" in the party.

"She has been running a parallel leadership campaign since the day after she lost the last one," Clement fumed. "When she doesn't get her way, this is the typical response from her. The ego and the constant demands, they just won't stop. It's always about Belinda."

I'm not sure how to square that accusation with the $100,000 Stronach gave Clement to help ease the crushing personal debt from overspending on his leadership campaign.

The roar of disapproval got louder when the editorial boards of Canada's newspapers weighed in with a thunderclap of next-day opinion.

The Calgary Herald: Belinda Stronach says her decision will restore integrity in politics. Hardly. Just two months earlier, Stronach was decrying Prime Minister Paul Martin's "failure of leadership," calling the government's complacency about the Canada–U.S. relationship a "political disgrace and an economic crime against Canadians" and saying the budget was "flawed and defective." Now, she's part of the team defending it. So much for integrity.

The Ottawa Citizen: Stronach's change of political stripes may help keep Martin in power for a few more months. But it does nothing to restore confidence in the Liberals, or in Stronach.

National Post: Stronach's move has temporarily bought her a bump up on the political pecking order. But in the long run, her defection may end up reflecting poorly on her personal credibility and will be remembered long after this Parliament is over. With a single stroke, she has harmed both her own reputation and the fortunes of her erstwhile colleagues.

The Montreal Gazette: The term "loose cannon" dates from the age of wooden navies. A massive metal gun, blasted or slipped loose from its place, could become utterly uncontrollable on a heaving, pitching deck. Such a gun, no threat to the enemy, became deeply dangerous to its own side, rumbling unstoppably across the deck, destroying everything it touched. Not a bad metaphor, then, for Belinda Stronach....

The Edmonton Journal: Not since Saul had his epiphany on the road to Damascus has there been a more vividly abrupt and profound about-face. And since we can surely rule out partisan divine intervention in an act Conservatives understandably view as betrayal, Stronach will have to talk fast and compellingly indeed to convince increasingly cynical voters she made her move for reasons other than personal ambition.

The Moncton Times & Transcript: With Tory defector Belinda Stronach now in charge of the Liberal government's "democratic renewal" plans, she should start immediately by shutting down Prime Minister Paul Martin's arrogant, cynical and bogus nation-wide campaign to buy voters with their own money.

The Windsor Star: If Stronach had any respect for her constituents, let alone the laws governing campaign financing, she would have resigned and run again in a by-election.

Frank Stronach could barely stomach the torch-and-pitchfork mob attacking his daughter.

"That was the saddest day of my life. The foul and dirty language which was hurled at her was like hyenas and vultures," he frowns. "The way she was treated was a very low thing. It was a great agony for her, but she did it for the right reasons."

Liberal MPs tried to counterbalance the condemnation with a group hug. Stronach received a standing ovation when she entered their caucus room for the first time. Former Conservative Brison came over, embraced her and ushered her to a seat beside him, presumably in the turncoat section. Deputy Prime Minister Anne McLellan took Stronach aside and said, "I always saw you sitting on the other side and you never looked comfortable."

Women in the Liberal caucus rallied to support Stronach against the negative opinion onslaught. McLellan had denounced media treatment of Stronach long before the defection. Sitting in her Ottawa office along with reporter Sean Gordon in the winter of 2004, I received a stern lecture on my profession's shortcomings in covering Belinda.

"I am appalled at the way you media have been focusing on what she wears, the suits she buys, the shoes she wears, how she looks," she scolded us. "Sorry, guys, but as a woman in politics, I've got to tell you I just think that's unacceptable at the beginning of the 21st century."

The day after the defection, McLellan once again rose to Stronach's defence, demanding an apology from Tory politicians, including Stephen Harper, for "sexist and misogynist" comments. She didn't get it.

STRONACH DIDN'T HAVE a lot of time to dwell on the scathing reviews. Ministerial briefing binders landed with a loud thud on her desk during her second day on the job, and she was told to get ready for a gathering of Cabinet the following morning. Emerging from that meeting, where insiders say she delivered an impressive address to ministers on her hopes for their future together, she was swarmed by reporters wondering how she was going to deal with MacKay and his potato patch sniffle.

"There's no question it'll be difficult and matters of the heart are emotional and complicated, but also very private," she said.

Privately, she was seething.

A couple hours later, with MacKay studiously examining his desktop in the Commons, Stronach was called to her feet by a Bloc Québécois MP for her first question as a minister. A warning from her father came to mind.

"I've always said the worst thing you can do is make some statement just to please the crowd or please a reporter," Frank Stronach recalls telling her. "There's nothing wrong if you don't know it to say 'I don't know it. If it's important I will dig into it and find the right answer.'"

Stronach's answer to the merits of creating an independent employment insurance fund echoed his advice. "It is a complex file. I will take the opportunity to study it and ensure that I make an informed decision that would be in the best interest of Canadian workers."

As she sat down, the Conservative bench erupted in jeers.

HUMAN RESOURCES AND Skills Development is not a sexy high-profile portfolio, at least not since the great HRDC boondoggle of the late 1990s when a billion dollars' worth of job-creation grants disappeared with little or no accountability.

Put to bureaucratic sleep after that scandal, it was a department that spent most of its time negotiating with provinces about workforce training, student assistance, employment insurance and tax breaks for caregivers of the terminally ill.

Chris White, her former chief of staff and a veteran of ministerial office management, says Stronach displayed a rare willingness to listen to her senior bureaucrats and told them to give her the good and bad news straight.

"When we got there, everybody was expecting a major screw up, but she was very deliberate on how she went about it. But there wasn't a shelf of stuff to accomplish," he admits. "Frankly, there's not a lot there."

Almost immediately, Stronach was confronted by the many overlaps between ministerial decision making and her family's multitude of business interests. She repeatedly excused herself from the Cabinet table to avoid potential conflicts of interest. She ducked on seemingly diverse discussions about the proposed Pickering airport, trade with Korea, regulations affecting the auto industry, satellite radio and even a debate on climate change with a tenuous connection to the steel industry.

With the summer recess in mid-June, Stronach took to the road to hand out job-training cheques to several provinces, her briefcase stuffed with never-ending briefing notes. She took a side trip to the Calgary Stampede, a rather brave sojourn given how the backlash to her defection was strongest in the West. She recalls getting only a few boos from the whooped-up crowds.

The cost of her leadership campaign was finally released by Elections Canada that summer. Hers appears to enter the history books as the most expensive bid ever, costing $5.3 million of which she personally paid $4 million. It might also rank as the costliest per-vote campaign ever, coming in at $150 per ballot cast in her name. Harper, by contrast, ended his $2.1 million race at $40 per vote.

AS SUMMER LIMPED into fall and the Martin government's solidarity with the New Democrats crumbled to set up a forced Christmas holiday election, the Honourable Belinda Stronach still had little to show for her desire to have a meaningful impact on government. As Paul Samyn of the *Winnipeg Free Press* noted in early September, her ministerial Web site featured one 438-word speech from July. The section on her personal Web site reserved for speeches and statements was empty.

Her signature accomplishment was to land a labour market agreement with hard-to-please Ontario. Three previous ministers had spent 10 years trying to nail down a deal without success. Stronach finally delivered the goods, a $300-million boost per year for the province to provide job training. It was warmly welcomed amid great fanfare by Ontario but, timing being everything in politics, news coverage of her announcement was dwarfed by Paul Martin's simultaneous giveaway tour in the fall, a $10-billion drop of pre-election goodies to buy voters with their own money.

As for the challenge of tackling democratic renewal, which Stronach had demanded as the price for her defection, it languished on a dusty shelf throughout her six months as a minister.

"Truth is, there were only so many hours in a day, and I had to hit the ground running. I wished we could've had it as higher priority in government because trust had deteriorated to such a low," she reflects now.

She talked about pushing for fixed election dates, but found the way partially obstructed by Ottawa MP Mauril Belanger, the government whip in charge of democratic "reform" who pointed out Stronach's territory was limited to democratic "renewal." Only in Martin's government could the two concepts be segregated into different departments. The foot-dragging was particularly hard to fathom given Martin's seminal address on the "democratic deficit" while serving as prime-minister-in-waiting in October 2003. It proposed revolutionary moves to enhance free votes, make committees more independent and pass more private member bills. In his most memorable line, Martin attacked the Jean Chrétien era as one where getting things accomplished depended on "who do you know in the PMO." Yet when Stronach proposed a massive push to sound out Canadians on ways to reverse the decline in voter turnout, which had dipped to an historic low of 61 percent in 2004, she was told the PMO knows best and to hold off.

"There was push-back from Langevin Block [the prime minister's business office]," agrees Chris White. "They knew it was an important file, but it was more a timing thing. The PMO wasn't ready to deal with consultations. It felt there were so many consultations taking place on so many files; this wasn't one they wanted to get into at that time."

Three days before the election force in late November, Stronach finally got Martin's green light to launch a

$900,000 fact-gathering blitz to find a cure for voter apathy. As it turned out, all they needed was a good excuse to cast a ballot. Two months later, voter turnout leapt 4 percent over 2004 as a motivated electorate rallied at the ballot box—to turf the Liberals from power.

THE JANUARY 23, 2006, fight for Newmarket–Aurora had all the makings of a defection referendum. Stronach distributed a two-page explanation for the floor-crossing as a primary piece of campaign literature. Her rival was consultant Lois Brown, the Canadian Alliance candidate Stronach had beaten for the merged Conservative nomination in 2004. If there was any doubt that Stronach was the raison d'être backing the Conservative campaign, Brown's slogan was "It's about TRUST."

Both sides knew their riding would be among the most closely watched anywhere. And, sure enough, an invasion of journalists hit the streets of Aurora, trying to decipher if the scarlet letter "L" would cost Stronach her seat. She was booked for daily hits with local and national broadcasters. Local, national and ethnic print media vied for interview time.

"This is the one riding that my readers want to know about," *Calgary Sun* columnist Rick Bell told a CBC documentary crew tracking Stronach. "It's bigger than anything. Bigger than Michael Ignatieff. Bigger than anything happening. They desperately want to see Belinda defeated."

I joined her on the hustings for a day just before Christmas. It didn't seem a particularly energetic effort at the time. Her office had less than a handful of volunteers on duty. The posted list of people willing to put up a Stronach election sign had but two names on it. Yet there was no doubting Stronach's celebrity status during a strip mall walkabout later that day. She needed no introduction and, despite my attempts to goad voters into raising the issue, nobody harrumphed her over the party switch. The keenest interest seemed to come from shopkeepers who hoped a bit of the legendary Stronach spending habit would rub off on their cash registers. Unfortunately for them, she'd left her purse at home.

Help for both camps was imported from far beyond the riding. A disgruntled worker from Stronach's leadership race flew in from Vancouver to help Brown campaign against her. Conservative headquarters dispatched MPs Rona Ambrose and Monte Solberg from Alberta, where their re-election was a given, to preach the party line. And Peter MacKay twisted the blade in Stronach's back a bit more by putting a ringing endorsement of Brown on her Web site.

But Stronach had a few ringers up her sleeve too, including her mother Friede, who worked the phones. Canadian Autoworkers' Union boss Buzz Hargrove, who had urged New Democrats to vote Liberal in ridings that might fall into Conservative hands, showed up to door-knock. It was an odd bedfellows scenario given that Hargrove was helping the heiress of a Magna auto-parts empire that remains defiantly anti-union. Ontario Health Minister George Smitherman helped her campaign while Toronto Maple Leafs forward Tie Domi and Toronto Argonauts quarterback Damon Allen added some sports star power to her lineup on the hustings. And right after celebrating New Year's Eve overseas, Frank Stronach showed up to help his daughter pound the pavement, proudly telling anyone who answered the door that his daughter wasn't a politician who could be bought and was therefore worth their vote. He didn't last long in the winter weather and developed a sudden preference for greeting people in warm, ice-free malls—at least until Wal-Mart took exception to his glad-handing inside their store and asked him to leave. On election night, Frank Stronach teased reporters he just might buy the local Wal-Mart and fire the management.

The all-candidate debates didn't hurt Stronach's campaign despite exposing her to the public wrath of those upset with the floor-crossing. Only one particularly aggressive heckler went after her over the defection, but Stronach was ready with e-mails that showed he'd ignored her offers to discuss it in a private meeting, and had, in fact, threatened to ambush her in public. He quickly sat down. Lois Brown's religious right beliefs became a factor in election forums too. After Stronach declared herself proudly pro-choice, Brown refused to state her position despite pressure from the audience. This was, no doubt, because there'd been a firm edict from the national campaign not to discuss the issue.

Brown's campaign was also hurt by Vote Marriage Canada, a religious group that unleashed a blitzkrieg of demon dialers on the riding to back its opposition to same-sex marriages while supporting Brown. But the group forgot to eliminate duplicates and delete those who had already been contacted, so indiscriminate and repetitive calls blanketed the local call zone and unleashed an angry torrent of nuisance complaints to Brown's office just days before the vote.

ON THE DAY OF DECISION, Stronach returned to the scene of her 2004 brush with defeat at Di Nardo's reception hall. The campaign had been encouraged by the positive reception in the riding, but remained gun-shy after the 2004 result. The team braced itself for another long night leading to a squeaker result. A concession speech was written and sitting on Stronach's desk. Television networks didn't know where to hook up their satellite trucks. If they powered up at Stronach's headquarters, what were they going to do if she lost? There'd be no coverage of Lois Brown, the giant slayer.

But this time Stronach knew she'd left nothing to chance. She had barely set foot outside the riding during the eight-week campaign bisected by the Christmas holidays. She'd been up waving at traffic most mornings. And on this final election-day push, she had been urging her supporters to vote until minutes before the polls closed at 8:30 PM, some 15 hours after she'd started the day shaking hands at the Aurora GO Train station. If she lost this time, she told her friends, it would not be for lack of effort.

But Stronach barely had time to bite her first fingernail before it was over.

"They called in the results of the first 16 polls very quickly," recalls campaign manager Kyle Peterson. "Ten went Tory last time and we took all 10. I knew it was over then. If you're winning polls you're supposed to lose, it's over."

An hour after the polls closed, CTV and CBC declared her the winner and Brown called in her congratulations. Stronach threw away her concession speech and headed downstairs where 500 locals were crammed into a room under surveillance by five television stations carrying her arrival live. She gave a smile to her children standing out of the limelight at the side of the room and waded through the mob to the sound of Bachman Turner Overdrive's "You Ain't Seen Nothing Yet." As her televised image hit the big screen in the Calgary Convention Centre, where Conservatives were gathering for their victory party, the crowd booed and hissed. Belinda was back. But at least Harper didn't have to worry about putting her in his Cabinet, one prominent Tory in the audience told me.

The re-elected MP did not dwell long on the local scene or even the sorry state of her adopted party. Her target was Prime Minister-elect Stephen Harper. On gay rights, women's issues, cities funding, the economy and national unity, "he will find in me an attentive and vocal critic," she warned, looking straight into the cameras. "Canada needs a government that looks to the future. So much of what defines Mr. Harper talks about issues that have already been extensively debated in the past, and where the country has already moved on to the next challenge—the right to same-sex marriage and the killing of the Kyoto Accord come to mind."

It didn't sound like a local MP claiming victory. Or even a one-issue critic asserting her place on the Opposition bench. It had all the makings of a manifesto aimed at bigger things to come. Minutes after Paul Martin announced his intention to step aside as Liberal leader, Stronach was the first contender asked the obvious question: "Are you going to run?"

"I just heard about this, and obviously I'd like to talk to Paul about it," Stronach stated. "But I've entered public life for the long term, to make a difference."

It was hardly a denial of interest.

Then again, Belinda Stronach had just done something many predicted would be difficult, if not impossible. She'd defected to a party that had lost power—and yet her victory margin soared to 4,800 votes from a narrow 689 votes just 18 months earlier. Newmarket–Aurora entered the election trivia books as the only riding in Canada where the Liberals reclaimed a seat from the Conservatives in 2006. And as for the minister who was put in charge of curing voter apathy, well, her riding recorded the sixth highest voter turnout in Canada. As a referendum on her defection, it was a thumbs-up landslide. But she'd won it big. And for Belinda Stronach, that means it's time to find another challenge.

Within a week, she quietly let word fan out across her political network. Assemble a team. Map out a theme. The Liberal leadership is accepting applications. And when Stronach spots an opportunity to become prime minister, well, b-b-b-b-baby, you ain't seen nothing yet.

— THIRTEEN —

"IT'S NOT YOUR TIME"

THE IMMINENTLY POWERLESS were exchanging goodbyes after the final Cabinet meeting of Paul Martin's defeated government on February 1, 2006. Belinda Stronach could be seen hugging defeated or demoted Liberal colleagues on the wraparound balcony of the prime minister's third-floor suite of offices. Back in those days, reporters could stake out the Centre Block Cabinet room and scrum departing ministers at both exits as they fled to the safety of their limousines. Terminating this access of evil was one of the first items of business under the new Stephen Harper regime, and what unfolded next may have been a motivating factor in his decision.

Watching the Cabinet break up from the corridor was veteran *La Presse* journalist Joel-Denis Bellavance. He's one of the most respected, connected and well-liked journalists on Parliament Hill with a signature gale of a laugh that, minutes earlier, had been ringing down the hallway. But as Stronach gathered her belongings and prepared to leave for her ministerial office, Bellavance's eyes narrowed behind wire-framed glasses.

"Is she really running?" he asked me.

I shrugged. With the abdication of all the heavyweights, she seemed set to enter the Liberal leadership race as a frontrunner.

"Go on, *seriously*? But she can't run. She doesn't speak French," he retorted. "Maybe I should test her. Here and now."

As Stronach edged toward the microphone, Bellavance moved in for the kill.

Was she running for the Liberal Party leadership? he asked her in clear, deliberate French even I could understand. Stronach froze, her composure a classic deer-in-headlights look.

"*En anglais s'il vous plaît*," she gasped.

Bellavance stood there mute, his face a mask. She could stay lost in translation as far as he was concerned. He wasn't about to repeat the question in English. For what seemed like minutes, but was probably no more than 10 seconds, awkward silence reigned until Stronach was saved by a different question in English from another reporter.

"That looked bad," Bellavance winced as he watched her disappear down the corridor in frantic conversation with her communications aide.

The televised encounter made afternoon politics shows in Ottawa and evening newscasts in Quebec, and underscored a near-fatal flaw in Stronach's fledgling candidacy. Bilingualism is no longer an asset for a federal party leadership hopeful. It's an imperative. And while Stronach had been taking French lessons in Ottawa and booked a week off in March for intensive immersion in Quebec City, there was no real hope of becoming proficient enough to contest the leadership in both official languages in time for the campaign.

THE HEIR APPARENT heavyweights were running away from the race in the weeks following Paul Martin's January 23 election night abdication of Official Opposition leader status, followed soon thereafter by his resignation as head of the Liberal Party. Before month's end, former Deputy Prime Minister John Manley declared himself disinterested in being Martin's replacement, followed the next day by U.S. ambassador and former New Brunswick Premier Frank McKenna. Former Newfoundland Premier Brian Tobin officially exited before Groundhog Day with former Jean Chrétien Cabinet Minister Alan Rock quickly following suit. For almost two months, the only declared candidate in the race was Martha Hall Findlay, ironically the same woman Belinda Stronach had displaced as Liberal candidate in Newmarket–Aurora the day she defected to Paul Martin's government. The once-mighty Liberal crown everybody used to covet seemed to have become filled with thorns overnight.

But Stronach wasn't sitting at home in Aurora knitting. A leadership exploratory committee had quietly begun its work. Officials were being signed up for paid and voluntary duty in every region. But one call gave Stronach pause to reconsider her entry a few weeks into the planning process. David Peterson phoned the MP he'd lured across the

Commons centre aisle to the Liberals just nine months earlier. *Was she going to contest the leadership?* he asked. Stronach said she was seriously considering a bid.

Don't do it, Peterson cautioned her. "It's not your time. If you go, sorry, I can't support you."

It had been a rough second-term restart for Stronach, placed back in the Opposition second row, facing former Conservative colleagues who gloated at every opportunity from the government side. She declined to ask a question for the first month in the House, primarily because her Transport critic duties were nowhere near one of Stephen Harper's top five priorities. The only excitement linked to her name was anticipatory speculation swirling over the date of her Liberal leadership launch. In the Commons, Belinda Stronach had become more a parliamentary curiosity than someone with political content.

That's why there were glum faces all 'round in the Gold Lounge on the second floor of the Château Laurier on the evening of April 5, 2006. Stronach communications assistant Maria McClintock was pulling names and phone numbers off her BlackBerry and writing them in a thick notebook. Stronach aide Lise Jolicoeur and strategist Mark Entwistle were fiddling with laptops on opposite sides of a portable bar. Nobody was saying much of anything. The highest-profile face backing her leadership campaign, former MP Reg Alcock, was studiously fixated on his BlackBerry. When I asked what was going on, he cast a wary eye at a cluster of businessmen within earshot and said that discussion would have to wait until the hotel found us a private meeting room.

He'd delivered my summons to attend an hour earlier. If I wanted a glimpse inside Belinda Stronach's leadership campaign as the guy writing her biography, this was a meeting I'd better not miss, he'd cautioned. Gosh, I thought when I arrived, the mood sure didn't fit a launch-planning party.

Alcock, a gregarious giant of a man with a voice that sounds like gravel rolling around in a cement truck, had lost his Winnipeg seat in a shocking upset three months earlier. He'd become an unabashed fan of Stronach's while serving in Martin's Cabinet as Treasury Board president. After Alcock had spent a full morning being grilled over plans to change the public service to prevent a repeat of the sponsorship scandal, Stronach had sent him a sympathetic note of support and offered to buy him lunch. They'd had a wonderful chat, and Alcock decided right there and then that there was more to her than many people thought. When she called in February, he volunteered to assist in plotting her route to the leadership convention.

Once inside the private suite, Alcock took the head of the table and started briefing me on a Stronach leadership team, which had been assembled coast to coast. Ontario was good, Quebec even better, he said. B.C. was taking shape. There were holes to fill in Alberta and Atlantic Canada, but she had the backing of Liberal MPs Ruby Dhalla, Joe Fontana, Tina Keeper and maybe even Cabinet Minister Raymond Chan. Former MPs Andy Savoy, Paul Bonwick and possibly Liza Frulla were on side, he said. Senators George Baker and Ron Zimmer were a lock. Staff from most regions were heading for a leadership planning session in Ottawa the next day. Everything seemed primed for launch. And then...

"She's out," Alcock said, not taking his eyes off his laptop's screen. "She's decided not to run. She's uneasy with a few things and is concerned about her kids. Everybody wants her to run, but it's too early. She is just deeply tired after two years going flat out in various campaigns." He paused to check his BlackBerry to type a couple messages with his thumbs. "She couldn't win," Alcock continued without prompting, "but I'm certain she'd finish second or third."

While being such a recent turncoat would've been fatal in almost any other race, being a brand new Liberal no longer meant having to say you're sorry in this odd campaign. All of Stronach's major rivals were misfits derived from other parties in other eras. Former Progressive Conservative MP Scott Brison. Former New Democrat Ontario Premier Bob Rae. Former Harvard academic Michael Ignatieff. Former Toronto Maple Leafs vice chairman Ken Dryden. Everybody had been something or somewhere else when Paul Martin was handed the Liberal leadership in late 2003, almost without a fight. Entering as a new recruit to the Liberal cause didn't seem to be a unique obstacle. But the candidate herself claimed another reason.

WHEN BELINDA STRONACH finally arrived from a workout in her new two-bedroom condo across the street, she grabbed a chair, ordered a dinner big enough for two, and turned to the group. She never acknowledged her decision directly, but jumped straight into the business of mothballing the campaign.

"Okay, let's do the logistics," she said.

Alcock recited a list of top provincial organizers who had to be contacted before the next day's news conference. She brushed off his suggestion of doing a conference call as "too impersonal."

"I'll call them one at a time." She paused to take a cell-phone call from daughter Nikki. "Any other meeting and I'd talk to you, but I can't right now," she told her 12-year-old daughter, who was searching for a specific DVD. "I'll call back in an hour."

Alcock pointed out a group of campaign officials who were heading for Ottawa for meetings the next day. A few had quit their jobs to work on the bid, he said.

"We'll have to make sure they're looked after," Stronach told him, making a notation in her binder.

Alcock pegged the cost of her unofficial campaign at $19,000 in expenses and $42,000 worth of travel and accommodation.

"That's not bad," Stronach noted. After settling on noon as the time for the news conference, her staff began brainstorming about her prepared text. Stronach stopped picking at a shrimp cocktail and interjected: "I'm not sure I'm going to use a text." She might do it straight from the heart.

There was an uncomfortable shifting in seats and averted eyes as the group appeared to recall the last time Stronach addressed a crowd without the teleprompter or a text. It had been two years, almost to the day, since she'd spoken to party faithful at the Conservative leadership convention with only a cheat sheet in her hand. It had been a modest success as a communications strategy. Okay, she decided after a few minutes, perhaps there'd be a short text to read before taking media questions.

"But we need to make sure there's a French translation," Stronach added.

Naturally. The Joel-Denis Bellavance encounter was never far from her mind.

What had driven her out of the race was not her failure at French. It was having the leadership decided by a delegated convention, she insisted. Some political parties elect their leaders through a direct membership vote, but the Liberals had decided to retain their age-old tradition of handing the crown to whomever lured the most delegates to their side on the convention floor. The membership in each riding elects 12 delegates to attend the early December convention with special delegate representation for Aboriginals, students and women. Those seeking delegate status could campaign for a particular leadership candidate, but it would be a secret ballot so there was no way of knowing how they voted with certainty. And if their choice did not survive the first ballot, the delegate's second choice was discretionary. Flawed as the process may seem, it's been the Liberal way throughout the party's convention history.

But Stronach didn't like it and had written an opinion piece for the *National Post* a few weeks earlier. A delegated process was undemocratic and open to abuse, she'd argued, but decided against sending it to the newspaper after reading a similar editorial argument by Ottawa MP David McGuinty, brother of Ontario Premier Dalton McGuinty. The voting method may not have been the only reason, but she insisted to her team that it was the key factor.

"It was not an easy decision," she said finally. "It's one of the toughest of my life, tougher even than my decision to join the Liberals. This wasn't as clear-cut. I could've run a very competitive campaign," she insisted, sensing my skepticism. "Seriously. I had a chance of winning, and the current system could've worked very well for me. I've got to go with my gut on this, to be free to express my opinion and ideas, and build a stage within the party. If it was one-member, one-vote, I'd have no problem being there. But we must have an open and democratic process."

It was strange, perhaps more so in hindsight a day later, that nobody in the room uttered a peep of warning that such a flimsy line of logic might crash into a wall of media skepticism. Nobody suggested Stronach might be better off hedging her main reason to include a desire to be with her family more or to become functionally bilingual or to wait for her Liberal roots to grow deeper into the party before setting out to become its leader. Perhaps they knew it would suggest human frailty, a gene the Stronach DNA is defiantly missing. Still, nary a discouraging word about her strategy was to be heard when the meeting adjourned after three hours. Stronach planned to fan out phone calls to key people at 11 AM the next day, a last-minute move to keep the decision secret. She would announce her decision at noon in the same National Press Theatre where Paul Martin had introduced his prized recruit just 10 months earlier.

"I need a good night's sleep," she said, yawning. "I just hope I'm still standing tomorrow afternoon."

WORD THAT STRONACH was exiting the leadership race leaked out hours before the scheduled announcement. CBC Television's Susan Bonner and CTV's Robert Fife hit the airwaves with the breaking news at the same time Canadian Press writer Sue Bailey filed an urgent story on the newswire. This wasn't the watertight seal that had kept her defection bombshell from reaching media. The element of surprise was gone, giving reporters time to prepare a line of attack to pick apart the explanation for her DOA candidacy.

For the second year in a row, a media frenzy was waiting for Stronach outside the Wellington Street entrance of the National Press Building. This time, she arrived alone as television cameras, newspaper photographers and a gaggle of curious reporters zeroed in on her emerging from a luxury sedan with her driver and bodyguard at the wheel. Other candidates had declared their intention to enter the race and had their launch barely covered, but Stronach exiting the race had both national networks carrying the announcement of her decision live. Sitting down in front of the same row of Maple Leaf flags she'd used as a backdrop for her defection, Stronach read a 10-minute statement of mostly English with some token stabs at French. Her eyes rarely left the text, and she delivered it scripted to the comma. So much for straight from the heart.

When she opened the floor to questions, it was a feeding frenzy. The first question, asked in French, was whether her unilingualism was the real reason driving her no-go decision.

"My French is better than you think," Stronach responded *en francais*. "And improving the quality of my French is a priority for me."

It didn't exactly flow effortlessly off Stronach's tongue, so television reporter Emmanuelle Latraverse took pity and switched to English to start hammering what became the persistent theme of the news conference: Why could Stronach not use a leadership quest to advocate Liberal Party reform? The logic seemed obvious: If you want a platform for new ideas, put yourself on the leadership podium. Put another way, how did seeking the leadership represent a muzzle to candid speech while standing on the sidelines could serve as a megaphone? Stronach never really explained that to anybody's satisfaction. Eyebrows arched as journalists repeated their questions from different angles and got back the same pre-packaged answer.

"Maybe some leadership candidates will bring that forward," she shrugged. "For me, the way I can have the greatest impact on the renewal of the party is to be free of the leadership."

Besides, she had other reform ideas to pursue, but promptly declined to list them. She told reporters she'd spent $30,000 exploring the bid, an inexplicable reduction from Alcock's calculation the night before. And then she was gone, her parting words perhaps more accidentally prophetic than politically promising.

"I'm not going anywhere," she said, before quickly correcting herself. "I'm not going away."

AFTER STRONACH LEFT the building, reporters swarmed Reg Alcock to fill the gaping holes in his candidate's rationale for leaving the race before it started. What, they wanted to know, would prevent a leadership candidate from pushing convention reform?

"Leaders end up in a bubble and end up getting managed day by day all the time," he said.

So was *he* planning to put her in a bubble?

"Look," he ducked, "she was getting into the routine for a traditional leadership, doing all the traditional things and she didn't like it."

But leaving because of convention rules that have been in place for decades? Come *on*, Reg.

"She is saying exactly what she feels about this. There's a disingenuousness about this that's absolutely real."

Reporters' brows furrowed at that one.

"The party wanted her to run, people in other camps wanted her in the race, but having been through it and having looked at it, she made a decision she did not want to go through this again," Alcock said, veering off the Stronach script. "She has a family and other interests in this life and made the decision she does not want to go through it."

So personal considerations did play into her decision? someone asked.

"I'm not going to add to her statement," Alcock said, "other than to say 'yes.'"

Stronach aide Lise Jolicoeur was getting nervous. Alcock was doing what press gallery veterans refer to as an "Andy Scott." It was christened in honour of the embattled former Liberal Cabinet minister, who found himself in hot water for comments about an overheard comment he'd made on an airplane. A tongue-tripping Scott had stayed in an endless scrum of reporters pleading a memory lapse until CBC reporter

Julie Van Dusen, having heard dozens of questions exhausted by his selective amnesia, finally asked the classic question: "What, did you get hit on the head by a rock or something?"

"I've got to get him out of here," said Jolicoeur, who had finally heard enough. Barely five-feet tall and weighing in at double digits, she reached over my shoulder and grabbed the towering 330-pound Alcock by his lapels to save him from his own mouth.

AS IT TURNED OUT, Stronach had a large organization primed to rumble. Natalie Duhamel, daughter of a former Liberal Cabinet minister and senator, was lead organizer for Manitoba.

"The campaign here was about a week from going full steam," she said. "We were ready to hit the ground selling memberships, but thought we'd hold back until she officially entered the race."

Quebec organizer Richard Mimeau, who guided Paul Martin's election and leadership campaigns, figures he had about 150 people committed to help Stronach run for the leadership in that province. He'd spent $8,000 hosting a pair of get-acquainted cocktail parties for Stronach, and says the reception in Montreal and Quebec City was generally positive. He was worried about Stronach's French language skills, though.

"If she had come to the first debate in Quebec and couldn't speak French and couldn't answer questions in French, it would not have been good for us," he allowed. "Being Conservative is one thing. Being Liberal, you have to speak French. I don't know if I could've held the team if she couldn't talk the language."

EIGHT DAYS AFTER quitting the race, Belinda Stronach strolled into the Magna Golf and Country Club on the southeast corner of the company's sprawling head office grounds. She was dressed in casual clothes, had her hair tied back in a small ponytail, and wore no makeup. She was miffed at the media reaction to her decision. Her stated reason for abandoning the Liberal leadership race a week earlier had been universally laughed off by pundits as the smokescreen for a lost campaign cause. And if that wasn't bad enough, caring for her children had been highlighted as the key reason for her decision. It's the one area of her life politics does not touch. During her election victory speech a couple months earlier, you would've had a tough time spotting Frank Jr. and Nikki in the crowd surrounded by family friends. It's partly for security reasons, but mostly to spare them the harsh glare of becoming a political prop. Yet here they were, cited by columnists (including me) and her own campaign strategist as a factor in her abdication.

It was obvious the decision had depleted Stronach's political zeal. Her future horizon in politics is confined to the Liberal Opposition bench where, at this writing, she's the critic for Competitiveness and the New Economy. It's hardly a top-five Harper priority and sure to keep her far from the media spotlight during Question Period. She's already talking about life beyond the political realm. Stronach wants to establish a think tank with representation from top sports, business and political realms to talk about ways to stretch the envelope on economic issues and global concerns. She's aiming to launch a Women's Fund in the fall of 2006, where investors could buy into a mutual fund of companies led by women entrepreneurs with a portion of the proceeds dedicated to helping girls' education programs. She's been approached to join a national speaking tour along with American entertainment executives like former Disney executive Michael Eisner. She is pushing a program to buy mosquito nets for poverty-stricken children in Africa. And, yes, she's quietly backing candidates to run for party executive positions at the Liberal convention who might embrace her reform ideas, including the one-member, one-vote concept at future leadership conventions.

But there's disillusionment in her voice at the sobering reality of being out of Cabinet after such a brief taste of holding the power to make change. She regrets not having had an impact on democratic reform as a minister. And Stronach knows she could be sitting on Opposition benches for a long time, thinking up questions her former fellow Conservatives won't answer. For someone with a short attention span who is hooked on profound and rapid change, hell beckons.

"I don't need this job," she says with a strong hint of resignation. "I had a hell of a good lifestyle before this. I made a hell of a lot more money, but I made a major commitment and am working hard at it because I care and I give a shit. I respected Paul Martin because he understood the global challenges facing Canada. David Emerson understands it too, but tell me another politician in that Parliament who's actually lived it, and it's not just coming out of a textbook."

Stronach pauses to order sparkling water, her drink of choice as she enters another intensive aerobic and flexibility training program to firm up a 130-pound body many keen (male) observers already argue is too thin.

"We don't have enough people that have had global business experience in government," she continues. "The biggest hurdle for them is: Why would I give up my freedom, why would I be put under the public scrutiny and get killed constantly to try and do some good? I spent the whole first year and a half of my career getting why, why, why? Why run for political office? It's not the money. It's not the power. I just want to do some change for the better. Why is that so hard for people to understand?"

She's had enough for the day. Stronach drains her glass of sparkling water and stands up to leave for an appointment with a constituent.

A few weeks later in the same clubhouse, I asked Frank Stronach about his proudest moment as father of Belinda Stronach. He looked across to the only other occupied table where his daughter was sharing a fruit plate with Toronto Maple Leafs hockey forward Tie Domi. She'd popped by to chat with her dad before he sat down for this book interview and to catch up with her hockey superstar pal who, his team having been eliminated before the playoffs, was getting ready to spend a cool early May afternoon on the golf course.

"I'm proud that she sacrificed a great life—you know vacations, ski trips, taking the private jet down south to Florida, whatever—that she exchanged that lifestyle for something where you'll get loads of critics and a little abuse is something." He pauses to give his daughter a wave as she heads out the back door for her nearby residence. "She was the head of the number two automotive-parts company in the world, we are number one sports betting company in the world. When you do that, you get access. I can call up any president in any country and can have great influence and still have privacy to a certain extent. I'm proud of her. She gave that up because she sincerely wants to serve her country for a number of years."

Exactly how many years, well, that's where the patriarch of the family struggles. He had always predicted his daughter would take only a five- to 10-year break from the company to test-drive politics. Her return as guardian angel of the Magna culture was always guaranteed because succession planning, to his mind, means All in the Family.

Where will Belinda be in 10 years? I asked him. It took exactly 30 seconds before Frank Stronach could figure out an answer.

"She will give it a try to change the system," he said, wincing a bit at giving such a flaccid answer after such lengthy contemplation. *But what,* I pressed, *if she fails?* Another pause as he stares at the tablecloth. "If she fails to change the system, then you must find some other ways." He offers no alternative beyond his own fallback position when he took a doomed run in 1988 as a Liberal candidate for a House of Commons seat. When he announced his plan, Stronach was chided by Bill Davis, a company board director.

"You're running for the wrong party in the wrong riding," he told Stronach.

"I know, Bill, but that's the way I am," Stronach recalls saying. "I know it's easier to flow with the wind, I know it's easier to swim downstream. But I have one advantage. If I don't get elected, I re-elect myself to the board of Magna."

For Belinda Stronach, exiting politics will always come with that same golden parachute and a clover-field landing.

— FOURTEEN —

HURRICANE
BELINDA

Belinda Stronach lives as the eye of a hurricane: a calm, drifting phenomenon blissfully unaware of the destructive havoc swirling beyond the blue. She never entirely meant it to happen, but her every action has had a profound reaction on Canada's political landscape in this millennium.

In three dramatic stages in just over two years, one of Canada's top business executives has morphed into the inadvertent Liberal godmother of today's Conservative government. Yes, you read that correctly. Belinda Stronach was a major factor in helping Stephen Harper win the last election.

Stage one was her quiet contribution to reuniting the Alliance and the Progressive Conservatives to create a new and credible Conservative rival to the Liberals as the Natural Governing Party.

"At a critical point in Canadian political history, she played a very central role in making a contribution to getting those parties together," argues former Conservative Prime Minister Brian Mulroney. "Stephen Harper won the January 2006 election in the autumn of 2003 with the reunification of the parties. Had that not happened, the Conservatives would not have won the last election."

Stage two was her entry into the 2004 Conservative leadership race, which brought a much-needed media frenzy to bear on a fledgling party trying to showcase its newfound moderation. She gave the contest a female contender representing youth, wealth and glamour while pitching a right-leaning business agenda minus the social conservative baggage. Had it merely been a finger wrestle between pale male Harper and perennial loser Tony Clement, the media would have ignored the race leaving the perception to linger that the new Conservatives were merely the old Reform Party under a fresh coat of Tory blue paint.

Finally, by crossing the floor she delayed an election the Conservatives were likely to lose until a time when they had a good chance to win.

The Conservative Party she abandoned in mid-2005 was freshly tarred with its near-unanimous opposition to same-sex marriage and seethed with self-righteous indignation at the scandalous revelations of the Gomery Inquiry. It looked excessively eager to take down the Liberal government after Paul Martin's promise to call a vote within 30 days of the final Gomery Inquiry report. It was led by a man considered geeky and aloof, even by his own MPs. But in the Stronach defection aftermath, a humbled Harper rallied his troops with an uncharacteristic group hug, reached out to Peter MacKay and set out to reconnect with party members.

David Peterson, the former Ontario premier whose accidental encounter at a May 2005 fundraiser set the defection in motion, recalls golfing at a fundraiser in mid-summer when a man approached, identified himself as the chair of the Conservatives' Quebec campaign and asked if he could shake his hand.

"You saved us," he told the former premier. "If we'd have had the election, we would've lost."

That man, Peterson says, was Michael Fortier, then Conservative campaign co-chair and now senator and minister of Public Works. Fortier's office did not respond to requests to confirm the conversation.

"He would not have done nearly as well," Bill Davis says of Harper's early push for an election. "She probably did [Harper] a favour by doing that, but I don't think it was intentional. I don't think the public was upset when the election was finally called because it was orchestrated in a fashion that Harper couldn't be blamed for. Had he gone earlier, he would've had to accept responsibility for doing something the majority of Canadians opposed."

Behind the scenes, senior Conservative operatives knew their platform was far from ready to contest the next election. All they had to run on was a Gomery backlash. They had a chance to win, but weren't ready to govern constructively if given a mandate. Several went to Harper and warned him they needed more time.

"Belinda caused all of us to pay more attention to each other," adds Senator Marjory LeBreton, a close confidante of the prime minister. "We started to talk to each other more. I don't know how it happened, but it happened. People with divergent views were accepted more. It was an amazingly unifying force in the long run. And we needed the validation of Gomery. If we'd gone in the spring, we wouldn't have had it."

After the Stronach defection and subsequent election delay, Liberals relaxed and went to their cottages for the summer of 2005, foolishly believing they had plenty of time to recover from Gomery and release a happy-face budget before heading to the polls in the spring of 2006.

But the Conservatives dived underground to tap credible candidates, raise money, fine-tune policy and map out a disciplined election strategy while Harper took a warm-up lap of the barbecue circuit. Strong foundations were being poured for a fall or winter campaign.

WITH THE GOMERY fact-finding report's release in November, Liberal dirt was spilled all over the public domain from a credible independent source. Tremendous damage was inflicted on a tainted Liberal brand without any help from their rivals. The Conservatives needed only to let the report speak for itself while they focused on developing their own positive plan to replace a tired, corrupted government.

When the election writ dropped on November 29, the Liberals didn't know what hit them. A focused, well-funded, tight-lipped and united Conservative rival roared out of the starting blocks. Their advanced state of readiness was, almost without doubt, the echo from Stronach's footsteps as she walked across the Commons aisle. Far from demonizing her, Prime Minister Stephen Harper should be shouting her praises from the rooftop of 24 Sussex Drive.

ON THE EVENING of May 17, 2006, Stronach was sitting in Ottawa's upscale Beckta's restaurant reflecting on the unexpected zigs and zags of her far-from-simple political life. There was a certain symmetry to the date. Exactly one year earlier she'd crossed the floor to join the Liberals.

"Know what you were doing a year ago this very minute?" I teased.

She didn't have to think hard.

"Freezing my ass off beside a CBC satellite television truck at Rideau Hall," she laughs. "I could barely talk by the time it started."

So...regrets?

"None, none, none," she insists. "I did the right thing for the right reasons." She says it with surprisingly fervent conviction. As for having an accidental hand in getting the Conservatives elected, she'd rather not buy the theory. "That certainly wasn't my intention."

This book concludes there are two distinct and almost irreconcilable Belinda Stronachs.

There's the apprehensive, tightly scripted one you've seen in the media or on stage with every strand of blonde hair coiffed into place, her clothes screaming Valentino, the message crafted by committee and her delivery rehearsed to the point where any hint of spontaneous spunk has been exorcized.

Then there's the version without makeup and her hair in a ponytail, wearing tastefully torn blue jeans, cursing like a sailor even with the tape recorder running, splitting a gut in the car while listening to a local personality's sappy vanity CD, slipping 10 grand to a hard-luck tragedy victim or proudly pointing out her kid's artwork beside a million-dollar Group of Seven original.

If you could pick the Stronach with greater potential for success in public life, it would be the human warmth projector. Unfortunately, it's the other split of her personality that's sitting in the House of Commons.

I'm still not sure why a naturally charismatic Stronach succumbs to a state of hyperventilating rigour mortis every time the spotlight shines in her direction. She can't be afraid of talking herself out of a paycheque, which she donates to charity anyway. There's a much more lucrative Plan B waiting just a five-minute walk from her front door in Aurora. Any opportunities for another leadership are a political lifetime away, so there's no worry about saying the wrong thing at this time. And yet, she seems incapacitated by free-flowing thought and stymied at spontaneous responses that taint her with the image of floundering dilettante.

Comedy show host Rick Mercer tells a story that confirms Stronach's place among the cardboard cut-outs in politics today. He woke up with a nasty bout of food poisoning on a chilly winter morning in early 2005. It was a shooting day for his popular television show *Monday Report*, so he dragged his grumbling stomach downstairs to the frozen Rideau Canal to meet Belinda Stronach, his feature guest of the week. She was made up to perfection and outfitted in political correctness, wearing a one-of-a-kind hockey jersey divided in half between the logos of her riding's two Junior A teams—the Newmarket Flyers and Aurora Tigers.

Waiting for the camera crew to set up, a drained Mercer sagged into one of the blade-equipped chairs they use to push children along the ice and struggled to engage Stronach in small talk. *So, he wondered, had she ever been on the canal before? Why yes, Stronach answered. Had she ever fallen down?* he asked. *Heck, yeah,* she cringed. In fact, she'd caught a crack in the ice, wiped out badly and landed with such force on her son's leg that she feared it might be broken. Mercer smiled. He could work with that. And the way he was longing for his sick bed, he hoped it would work on the first take.

With cameras rolling and Stronach gamely pushing Mercer along in a kiddie sled, he asked her if she'd been on the canal before and if she'd ever done a butt plant on the ice. *Sure she'd been here before,* Stronach answered. But in lieu of her humanizing crash onto Frank Jr's leg, she launched into a speech about the tourism impact Winterlude celebrations had on the national capital region. Mercer rolled his eyes. Back in the editing studio a few days later, he debated killing the sleepy segment outright, but reluctantly pushed it into the last half of the show. "We've never done that with a feature guest before."

THE FACT SHE says nothing too often and something only when it's in a script leads to the most persistent question about Belinda Stronach: Is she smart? You don't hear that question directed at most multi-millionaires who have graced the list of the world's most important business personalities. Their intelligence is taken for granted. But because it's such a common curiosity about Stronach, it suggests doubt, that somehow this is a Barbie doll without a brain instead of someone *Time Magazine* christened a global influence.

After spending a dozen hours with her and dozens more in the cloistered world of her friends and family, I'm of two views. If "smart" means knowing the inner workings of car door assemblies or the secret to wowing large public gatherings with searing worldly insights, nope. She'll never upstage Liberal MP Michael Ignatieff in a debate on ways to resolve the Sunni-Shia conflict in Iraq. Prime Minister Stephen Harper should never lose sleep preparing to cross swords with Stronach on the fairest equalization formula for the have-not provinces.

But one-on-one with people of all demographics, particularly those who need help and a compassionate connection, she's a genius. Her election campaign teams have one goal in mind when they put her in the field: Meet people. Get Stronach to chat up 1,000 voters and she'll land 800 votes. The closest I've come to seeing this sort of instant likeability in campaign action was Alberta Premier Ralph Klein—and that was during his drinking days. Even beyond the doorstep she inspires incredible lasting loyalty from most of those in her orbit. Her household helpers have all held the same jobs for 15 years. When she crossed the floor, only two of a dozen senior Conservative campaign volunteers left her side. The rest declared themselves Stronach soldiers first, party faithful second and marched in lockstep with her into uncertain turncoat territory. Even some of the most successful Conservative leaders of the last generation—Brian Mulroney, Bill Davis and Mike Harris—refuse to speak ill of an MP who strayed so spectacularly from their party into the enemy's fold.

Still, she can bring out the worst in some people.

Stephen Harper's mercurial paranoia never loomed larger than his treatment of Stronach. Despite her work in reunifying the party and legitimizing the leadership race, his people were dispatched to Aurora to try and deny her the party nomination. Whether they acted on his personal orders is unclear. But after his leadership victory, Harper seemed to do everything in his power to neutralize what he perceived as a future rival through isolation, marginalization and humiliation. They were mostly small irritants, but they added up to a coordinated putdown strategy in Stronach's mind.

Then there's the inexplicable bitterness in Peter MacKay's response to Stronach's defection. While MacKay was only too eager to forsake a leadership-crowning promise to David Orchard not to merge with the Alliance, he still cannot forgive a lover for merely shifting seats between a Conservative and Liberal Party of roughly similar ideologies. What's worse, he responded to her discreet silence about their shattered relationship by calling in the satellite trucks to showcase his bruised ego on national television. And what kind of man declares his fervent attachment to a woman's children in one breath and rates his loyal dog ahead of their mother the next? It was a public reaction so shallow and self-serving, one has to think MacKay will leave politics without another party leadership to call his own.

And yet, if the real Stronach has such profound negative or positive impacts on people, how to explain the blank thoughts about her from those who have shared her life? Consider this parting exchange in an interview with former husband Don Walker, a man Stronach still puts inside a very tight circle of trust.

MARTIN: Are there any memories that should be in this book about you and Belinda which define her and just have to be part of her story?

[Long pause]

WALKER: Nothing really jumps out at me. She's very personable and likes to have fun and works hard. She's a bit of a visionary. Any particular stories? I can't think of any.

Just as baffling are the number of close friends who say roughly the same thing. Maple Leafs hockey player Tie Domi, for example, has been a close friend of Stronach's for years, but drew a zero at any character-defining experiences.

"I just think people would be surprised how shy a person she is," he shrugged. "Um, I don't really know what else to say."

Okay, it might be they're protecting private recollections with an amnesia of convenience. Or it could mean there's nothing to recall, that Stronach doesn't register through signature moments. Still, it's hard to believe because as someone who's been but a passing flicker in her life, I have no trouble recalling incidents offering a glimpse into her character.

On the evening of her clash with Stephen Harper, where he'd read her the riot act and warned her she'd never be a party leader, Stronach was trying to shake off a reflective glumness at a gathering of staff, colleagues and media. After the dinner wrapped up and the group poured out on Elgin Street, Stronach spotted a candy store called Sugar Mountain.

"Pez for everybody!" she hollered. Dragging the entire gang inside the store, she bought a round of candy dispensers. "Think I should get this for Harper?" she smirked, holding up Spongebob Squarepants, a cartoon character some groups accused of being gay. "Hell, why not?" She'd been beat up, but was clearly not beaten.

Two weeks later, I ran into Stronach on an Ottawa street corner. It was the evening of her defection. She was pale and almost zombie-like with bags under her eyes no amount of makeup could mask, but was gamely heading toward the CTV studios for a final interview to finish off a long day in the media glare. After that, she was flying to Aurora where constituency office staff waited for her explanation.

She forced a smile as we intersected and paused to chat. I warned her my next day's column on her would be brutal and that western Canada felt particularly aggrieved by her political switcheroo. She looked at the sidewalk for a moment and patted my shoulder before moving along.

"You gotta do what you gotta do. I have no problem with that," she said. "But we should have a drink sometime. There's more to this story than you know."

You can judge for yourself, but perhaps this book shows that was indeed the case.

A former adviser, still bitter about her decision, takes a tarnished view of Stronach's halo.

"She's got rich-girl disease," he argues. "She takes a trip to Africa when she should be in French immersion. She has a very short attention span. She'll drop everything and go onto something else and leave someone else to clean up the mess. She flits from idea to idea and, while some might say you're entrepreneurial, others might say you need discipline."

Her pal Bonnie Shore sees that attention deficit much differently, arguing that Stronach is turned on by fear and is always looking for new places to find it.

"If you've ever seen her ski, you'd understand. She skis like a mad woman," Shore says. "She is a beautiful skier, almost world class. She takes on a mountain of moguls like they're not there. I asked her. 'Don't you get scared?' She says, 'Yeah, but that's the good part.' It's not that she's not human. She's as scared as any of us, but it pushes her, motivates her to drive on until she conquers it. She loves the chase more than the win."

It's a valid insight. Stronach set out as a teenager chasing the Magna chair job. Then she went after husbands. Then she wanted the Magna CEO spot. Then she sought the presidency. Then she hunted the Conservative leadership. Then she fought to be elected and re-elected as an MP. Finally she contemplated the Liberal leadership. Every time she caught something or finished lunging at a target, she quickly switched to something else.

Until now.

Now, Belinda Stronach has a problem. The Liberal road ahead seems likely to be an Opposition dead end for years.

The only escape route is a been-there, done-that retreat to her father's Magna executive offices.

But she won't sit still. She can't. She has a time-sensitive personality and is hooked on constantly changing her world before she leaves it. Mortality, you see, preoccupies Stronach. It was no accident she was the oldest person in her ministerial office. She craves youth. It's not that she fears death so much as she appreciates the shortness of life. Unlike her father, who plans to live until he's 150 years old, Belinda Stronach is acutely aware that her best days are passing by and resolves to make them all count.

Former top aide Mike Liebrock recalls campaigning in a seniors' home during the 2004 election when a resident pointed to a Countdown Clock on the wall. It was used to tick down the hours to important events at the lodge, but one lady clutched Stronach's hand and urged her to get her own clock. That way, she said, Belinda Stronach could count down the 15 years left before she could move into the lodge as a minimum-aged senior. Most people would grin and shake it off. But Stronach was mortified at the thought that the alleged "golden years" are rushing toward her so quickly when so many personal challenges had yet to be attempted.

MARTIN: You always talk about looking back on your life from the vantage point of your 80th birthday and here you are on the eve of your 40th.

STRONACH: "I'm halfway there. My God! My God!" [She put her head on the table.]

MARTIN: Are you happy where you are? Are you satisfied?

STRONACH: "I'm not satisfied, but I'm happy. Know what that means? It means I'm going to become more intense about things. I'm going to become more insane about time and priorities. I'm very disciplined. I work hard, but I go out and do life with a lot of intensity. The closer I get to 80, the more intense I'll get. There'll be a lot of things when I'm 60 I'm not going to be able to do any more."

MARTIN: So do you dread aging?

STRONACH: I don't know about that. Being 40 is the new 30. Ask me when I'm 50. It's all about attitude and energy. I have a lot of energy and run half my friends into the ground. They think I'm insane, but it's just attitude. It sounds so basic, but you've got to love what you do.

ON FEBRUARY 14, 2006, the only flowers at Belinda Stronach's residence were for her daughter. Her son, Frank Jr., was in Turin, Italy, attending the 2006 Winter Olympic Games with Johann Koss. Stronach was between male admirers and had dinner booked with her mother and daughter at the Joia Restaurant, a casual joint in Aurora serving the best Italian food around. She was supposed to be joined by Don Walker, but he'd cancelled. Stronach's scheduling assistant figured the request to include "Don" meant this visiting author instead of Magna's new CO-CEO, so that's how I was inadvertently invited to spend Valentine's Day dinner with three generations of Stronach women, the only male at the table.

Nikki and her mother arrived on the stroke of six. Punctuality is something of a religion with Stronach. She expects it of others, even if she doesn't always practise it herself. Friede Stronach showed up 25 minutes late, just as her daughter impatiently contemplated ordering food without her. Her mother has a lingering Austrian accent and light blonde hair. She looks and plays the part of the doting grandmother and concerned mother well. She has no trouble getting Nikki engaged in talk about horses and has an obvious motherly affection for her daughter.

Dinner had been cleared and conversation on a wide variety of topics had run its course when Friede Stronach turned to me.

"So, you're doing a book," she said. "What's it about?"

I looked at Belinda Stronach quizzically, trying to figure out if writing her biography was a deep, dark secret to be kept from her parents. She shrugged.

"Um, it's about your daughter," I confessed.

"I know *that*," the mother said with a patient smile. "But is there enough to write about? Her story isn't finished yet."

It's true that Stronach is still very much a work in progress. In a political life that has spanned only two years, she's fought a leadership contest, been elected and re-elected in her riding, triggered a national firestorm as a government-salvaging defector, served in Cabinet and backed away from her second party's leadership race only at the last minute. For someone who was supervising a Magna essay-writing contest just 10 years earlier, that Herculean leap could be driven only by lustful ambition.

Still, it's a widely held belief in Ottawa that Stronach is a fading flash in the political pan as she languishes in the uneventful obscurity of the Liberal Opposition benches. Speculation abounds that Frank Stronach used her as a Trojan horse to storm the only realm to which Magna's millions denied him a red-carpet entry. With two party leadership possibilities passing her by, this theory suggests the father will lose interest in the daughter's parliamentary pursuits faster than he ditched plans for Magna Air with its Mile-High-Club bedrooms for ocean-jumping executives.

But those who know Belinda Stronach well insist she is driven by a genuine sense of public duty, a woman of intellectual substance, spiritual compassion and gifted insight who can connect in an instant and have a lingering impact on almost everyone she meets. She sees the best and doubts the worst in people, judging character without prejudice or malice unless and until their negatives become impossible to ignore. She is someone of modest ego who abhors gossip, shuns sycophants and seems genuinely baffled that anyone would find her public and private life at all interesting or book-worthy. She is grateful to have been born into extraordinary wealth, believing it comes with a serious social responsibility to do good deeds. The return to the jet-setting hedonistic lifestyle of a blonde billionairess will just have to wait until Stronach solves a global scourge or two.

It's doubtful she'll ever get to write her own Magna essay version of "As Prime Minister I Would…" from first-hand experience as a tenant of 24 Sussex Drive. But her genes contain a fascinating mix of her father's humanity-saving energy and her mother's well-grounded compassion. Stronach will inherit the monetary means to do even more dramatic things with her insatiable drive after losing interest in the banal world of federal politics. She is a fortuitous accident of birth, delivered with a silver spoon in her mouth and a rattling desire to do something big with it in her hands.

Friede Stronach is right. Her daughter's story isn't finished yet. She has already brought wealth, glamour, sexuality, tension, treason and heartbreak to the male-dominated, blue-suited drudgery of Parliament Hill.

For Belinda Caroline Stronach, the next mountain awaits.

INDEX